Black troops guarding a stagecoach
(Records of the Office of the Chief
Signal Officer, RG 111).

Afro-American History: Sources for Research

Afro-American History

Sources for Research

EDITED BY ROBERT L. CLARKE

 HOWARD UNIVERSITY PRESS/Washington, D.C./1981

This Special Edition
published by Howard University Press for the
National Archives Trust Fund Board
National Archives and Records Service
General Services Administration
Washington, D.C.

Printed in the United States of America.

Library of Congress Cataloging in Publication Data
National Archives Conference on Federal Archives as Sources for Research
    on Afro-Americans, Washington, D.C., 1973.
    Afro-American history.

    (National Archives conferences; v. 12)
    Papers and proceedings of the conference held June 4-5, 1973 sponsored by the
    National Archives and Records Service.
    Includes index.
    1. Afro-Americans—History—Sources—Congresses. 2. Afro-Americans—
History—Archival resources—Congresses. I. Clarke, Robert L. II. United States. National
Archives and Records Service. III. Title. IV. Series: United States. National Archives and
Records Service. National Archives conferences; v. 12.
E184.6.N37 1973   973'.0496073   80-19197
ISBN 0-88258-018-3

vi

NATIONAL ARCHIVES CONFERENCES

VOLUME 12

Papers and Proceedings of the Conference on Federal Archives as Sources
for Research on Afro-Americans

June 4-5, 1973
The National Archives Building
Washington, D.C.

Preface

The National Archives Conference on Federal Archives as Sources for Research on Afro-Americans was held on June 4 and 5, 1973, the twelfth in a series of conferences sponsored by the National Archives and Records Service. The choice of Afro-American history as the subject of this conference seems particularly appropriate at this stage in our national life. Interest in the role played by Afro-Americans in our nation's past has increased dramatically over the past two decades, as has the interest in primary sources that shed light on that role.

We at the National Archives have welcomed this growing awareness of the research potential of original materials. The archives of the United States are, in a sense, the collective memory of the nation, and within these permanently valuable records of the federal government are rich reservoirs of information on the history of Afro-Americans. This volume, and the conference that generated it, represent one way in which the National Archives has attempted to introduce researchers to the potential of our holdings.

Robert L. Clarke, National Archives specialist in Afro-American history, directed the conference and edited this volume. As a researcher and a reference specialist, he knows well the archival records that bear on Afro-American history and the needs of researchers for guides into their abundance. It is his hope, and mine, that the publication of this volume will stimulate research on Afro-Americans, thereby contributing to a better understanding of our nation's past.

Robert M. Warner
Archivist of the United States

Contents

III

The Multipurpose Use of Federal Archives

IV

Related Records and Projects

V

Afro-American Social History
Based on Federal Archives:
The Family

VI

Assessment
and Prospects

List of Illustrations

Picture credits: Unless otherwise noted, the illustrations reproduced in this volume are from National Archives records and are identified by record group or file number.

Introduction

Afro-Americans were a part of the history of the Americas long before there was a United States, but until recently historians had neglected their story. The emphasis of historians had been on the study of a monolithic, melting pot nation, and the segments—political or ethnic—that make up the whole had been studied less than the whole. But with few exceptions, historians and social scientists had not included Afro-Americans in studies that were obviously incomplete without them. Even when Afro-Americans were included, many writers saw them through their own cultural biases, deliberately or subconsciously.

Fortunately, the emphasis of historians and social scientists has changed to one which reflects the cultural diversity of America, and Afro-American history has become a serious topic for major research. The purpose of the National Archives Conference on Federal Archives as Sources for Research on Afro-Americans is to encourage this long-overdue research.

There were two specific conference objectives: to inform scholars and researchers about the useful research materials available in the National Archives and to give researchers an opportunity to suggest ways in which the National Archives could facilitate better use of these records.

The papers in this volume were delivered in the theater of the National Archives Building on June 4 and 5, 1973. They appear in the order in which they were originally presented. The papers were followed by comments or questions from the floor; these comments have been summarized and follow the papers of each chapter. Some of the presentations have been updated by the authors to reflect additional research in the years between the conference and the publication of this volume.

I am indebted to a number of people who contributed their time and support to making the conference a success. John Hope Franklin made suggestions during the initial planning, and Elsie Lewis, Leon Litwack, Andrew Billingsley, and Edgar A. Toppin assisted with the program. John E. Bryne and Steven Carson took care of the innumerable details necessary to organize such a conference. Debra Newman and Deborah Mariner were invaluable assistants. Walter Robertson, Jr., then executive director of the National Archives; James E. O'Neill, deputy archivist of the United States; and James B. Rhoads, former archivist of the United States, were unstinting in their advocacy and support of the conference.

Finally, my thanks go to Betty Cooks, who made a significant contribution by assisting with the editing and preparation of the papers for publication.

Robert L. Clarke
Conference Director

Afro-American History:
Sources for Research

Opening Remarks:
The Journal of Negro History
and the National Archives

W. AUGUSTUS LOW

The *Journal of Negro History* is the greatest single printed source for the authentic, scholarly story of blacks in America. It is both a great mirror and mosaic of the black heritage. For more than a half century, it has attempted to erase myths and stereotypes and to correct past omissions in historiography. The journal has sought to give rightful recognition to the significance of blacks in American history.

Since the first issue of the journal appeared in January of 1916, a total of 686 issues in sixty-three volumes have been published consecutively. Most of the issues have consistently followed a basic format, which includes articles, documents, book reviews, and bibliographical essays.

The feature article in the journal's first issue was written by the founder and editor of the journal, Carter G. Woodson, a great historian. In gathering information for this article, "Negroes of Cincinnati Prior to the Civil War," Woodson did not use the National Archives; it simply did not exist then. In contrast, Monroe Billington of New Mexico State University relied heavily upon the Truman Papers in the Harry S. Truman Library in Independence, Missouri, to write the feature article in a 1973 issue of the journal, "Civil Rights, President Truman and the South." The same issue of the journal also contains an article by Victor B. Howard that is based in part on federal archives. The article, "The Black Testimony Controversy in Kentucky, 1866-1872," demonstrates good use of the Freedmen's Bureau records (Record Group 105).

In a sense the period between the appearance of the first and the 1973 feature articles reflects the tremendous growth in the use and importance of archival sources in our nation. During the intervening years, many more writers, including myself, have tapped the rich resources of the National Archives to write articles for the journal.

The Freedmen's Bureau led to my earliest use of the National Archives and to the publication of my first article, "The Freedmen's Bureau and Civil Rights in Maryland," in the *Journal of Negro History*. I had become interested in the Freedmen's Bureau and its operation in Maryland after a long conversation with John Henry Nutter, a senior citizen, who was then in his nineties. He lived in Worchester County, Maryland, and was the first and oldest living graduate of Morgan State University, which was then called the Centenary Biblical Institute. That conversation with Nutter provided me with valuable oral history. In seeking materials on the Freedmen's Bureau, I was inevitably drawn to visit the National Archives. My visit proved to be fruitful, for the ample information that I found at the archives formed the basis of my article.

Many more authors have used National Archives records in researching articles they were to write for the *Journal of Negro History*. William Tuttle of the University of Kansas contributed an article entitled "Congested Neighborhoods and Racial Violence: Prelude to the Chicago Riot of 1919." His sources of documentation for the article included the records of the Federal Mediation and Conciliation Service (Record Group 280). The article appeared in the October 1970 issue.

Myra Himmelhoch, a diplomatic history student at Washington University, St. Louis, Missouri, contributed an article based on archival sources that appeared in the July 1971 issue of the journal. The article, "Frederick Douglass and Haiti's Môle Saint Nicolas," discusses the Môle, a piece of real estate that the United States had an interest in for probable use as a naval base. Frederick Douglass was then the minister to Haiti. That same issue of the journal included "Alabama's Soldier Experiment, 1898-1899" by William B. Gatewood, Jr. Gatewood pointed out that bibliographical data found in federal archives contribute to a better understanding of the work blacks performed in a predominantly rural southern state. He stated "biographical data contained in the regiment's records indicate that a majority of the recruits had been employed as porters, mechanics, caterers, cooks, insurance agents, and barbers, rather than farmers or farm laborers." Gatewood also cited as sources the clothing accounts of the regiment of the Third Alabama Colored Infantry, United States Volunteers, whose records are preserved in the Records of the Adjutant General's Office (Record Group 94).

While doing research for her article, "Black Merchant Seamen of Newport, 1803-1865: A Case Study in Foreign Commerce," which appeared in the June 1972 issue of the journal, Martha S. Putney examined the records of the U.S. Customs Service. She found crew lists that contained various kinds of information that documents the role and presence of blacks in commercial and whaling activities from the port of Newport, Rhode Island. The lists reveal information such as name, age, place of birth, personal description, and the most recent place of residence of each crew member for each voyage. From the personal description column, which denotes complexion and hair, Putney resolved the intriguing problem of identifying black crew members. She writes:

> Occasionally when the words 'African' or 'sable' or 'colored' or more frequently 'black' or 'mulatto' were found in the complexion column, there was no question about the man's race. The same would be true if the column carried the notations 'slave' or 'free yellow' or if the hair of a person was described as 'black woolly,' 'grey woolly' or just 'woolly.'
>
> When words such as 'copper,' 'dark copper,' 'dark,' 'darkish,' 'yellow,' 'light brown,' 'brown,' 'dark brown,' 'clear brown,' 'inclining to brown,' 'brown and ruddy' or 'dark and ruddy' were inserted under complexion and the notation in the hair column contained no more revealing data than 'dark' or 'black' or 'curly,' a valid assumption would be that these individuals so described were black also. This assumption is strengthened by the circumstance that some of the same lists which contained these descriptive traits characterized other members of the crew as 'fair,' 'rather fair,' 'light,' 'rather light,' 'fresh,' 'rather fresh,' 'florid,' 'light but sun-tanned,' 'dark but sun-tanned,' 'sallow,' and the like. These latter adjectives undoubtedly categorized the nonblack crew members although many blacks could be so depicted. As regards those crew members who were described as yellow with dark or black hair, a check was made in the name column and if the latter was of western or African origin, such an individual was considered black.

As shown in the pages of the *Journal of Negro History,* the National Archives can be used effectively and imaginatively in writing good history. This conference will focus upon the numerous uses of archival records relating to blacks. In all of its great and magnificent diversities, dimensions, varieties, and nuances, black history has been enriched and delineated by sources from these federal archives.

I

Federal Archives: Their Nature and Use

Saving Federal Records for Research

HAROLD T. PINKETT

Above the classic porticos on the main facades of the National Archives Building are inscribed the words Archives of the United States of America. The inscription is not meant, of course, to indicate that the building is the repository of all archival materials in the United States, but rather is designed to mark the building as the archival treasurehouse of the United States government.

What are these archives? Briefly defined, they are the permanently valuable records that have been created or accumulated by the federal government for its official purposes. The records have two principal values. First, they contain essential evidence of the organization and operations of the government. As such they show administrative responsibility and performance; document official procedures, policies, and precedents; and protect the rights of the government and its citizens. Second, the records constitute a basic source of historical information about the American people and their environment. Accordingly, records of this character become important sources for research. How these records enter the documentary preserve designated as archives is the theme of this paper.

This documentary preserve had its beginning in 1774, when the First Continental Congress chose a secretary to keep a journal of its proceedings and to be custodian of its official papers. These official papers and subsequent records generated by the United States government during the next 160 years yielded a varied and voluminous archival product, in spite of the lack of a government-wide agency entrusted with their evaluation, care, and use. During this period, each federal bureau usually retained custody of its own records and in effect decided what documents should be kept permanently.

Meanwhile, the importance of government records for nongovernment use, such as historical research and related investigations, became more widely appreciated. The value of government records was clearly evident to American historians who, by the end of the nineteenth century, were making increasing use of the records of foreign governments preserved in the British Public Record Office in London and in other European archival institutions. Herbert Osgood and Charles Andrews, for example, were expounding to their professional colleagues new approaches to American colonial history based upon extensive research in the archives of Great Britain. In 1910 the American Historical Association noted the lack of a system to preserve federal records and adopted a resolution describing them as "muniments of our national advancement and materials which historians must use in order to ascertain the truth."[1] The association petitioned the Congress of the United States to establish in Washington, D.C., "a national archives depository" where records of the federal government might be properly preserved and made available for research as well as for administrative purposes. Shortly thereafter, other historical and patriotic societies expressed this concern. The concern of such societies, the administrative needs of the government, and the example of leading foreign governments gave impetus to the movement that led to the establishment of the National Archives as an institution in 1934.

By that time, federal records that had been designated to be housed in the National Archives of the United States were varied groups of documentary materials that had been reduced by losses incurred during frequent transfers from one place to another, and by the depredations of thefts, fires, dampness, heat, rodents, and insects. In spite of these losses, however, the materials that had accumulated during a century and a half of national government were immense and of great value for administrative and research purposes.

The establishment of a national archival agency made possible the systematic examination and appraisal of all federal records and the selection of those records that deserve to be retained permanently. This appraisal, conducted under the direction of the archivist of the United States, began with a survey of several million cubic feet of records accumulated by federal agencies in the District of Columbia and in the states. From this survey, the first groups of records were chosen for transfer to the National Archives Building, beginning in 1935. The variety and volume of these documents defied any effort to categorize them precisely. They included memorials and petitions sent to Congress by ordinary citizens, as well as messages sent to that body by presidents; memorandums of obscure bureau clerks and reports of departmental heads; case files relating to pension claims of veterans and battle reports of the Civil War; court papers with depositions of forgotten persons and decisions of famous jurists; routine weather reports and studies of earthquakes; and maps of city squares and charts of vast sections of the public domain. These records were created and accumulated by all elements of the federal government—the Congress, president, executive and regulatory agencies, and the courts. In February 1936, after the first records had been transferred to the new National Archives Building, Secretary of State Cordell Hull, chairman of the National Archives Council, called the repository a "home of history" and envisaged its task as one of preserving the "endless drama" of American democratic strivings.[2]

Within a decade after 1935, some 700,000 cubic feet of federal records had been appraised permanently valuable and transferred to the custody of the National Archives establishment; the majority of these documents were more than fifty years old. Also during this period, new legislation and regulations allowed the agency to develop an accessioning program that reflected a more precise definition of records, greater encouragement of regular transfers, and incipient development of appraisal standards. The Disposal Act of 1943 defined records as "all books, papers, maps, photographs, or other documentary materials, regardless of physical form or characteristics, made or received by any agency of the United States government in pursuance of federal law or in connection with the transaction of public business and preserved or appropriated for preservation by that agency or its legitimate successor as evidence of the organization, functions, policies, decisions, procedures, operations, or other activities of the government or because of the informational value of data contained therein." This definition encompassed traditional records but emphasized responsibility for evaluating maps, photographs, sound recordings, and other nontextual materials for possible preservation. The legislation also authorized comprehensive schedules for evaluating records: records of temporary value could be destroyed after specified retention periods and records of permanent value could thereby be systematically segregated and preserved as archives. The legislation was important to the development and implementation of records administration plans. It stressed the idea that the disposal of valueless records is only an aspect of preserving valuable records and making them useful.

APPRAISAL REPORT ON TRANSFER OFFER

Job No. NN-374-128   March 11, 1974

Custodian: Equal Employment Opportunity Commission

Address: 1800 G Street, N. W.
           Washington, DC   20506

Person with whom to confer: Gary Papritz, Records Management Officer
                               Room 1138 (Phone 343-8409)

(1) Identification of Records:

Records of the Equal Employment Opportunity Commission created in
connection with EEOC litigation against the American Telephone and
Telegraph Company and its subsidiaries before the Federal Communications
Commission, 1971-73. This case, referred to by some EEOC officials as
the most important proceeding in the Commission's history, resulted in
an agreement in which the Company agreed to pay over $20 million to
those of its employees who had presumably been discriminated against in
terms of promotions and career advancement opportunities. These records
include verbatim transcripts of the oral proceedings before FCC during
most of 1972 and the exhibits introduced by EEOC to support its
contentions. Most of these exhibits, which make up the bulk of these
records, were chosen from the estimated 100,000 pages of documents
received from the 22 different Bell System companies in response to the
detailed interrogatories of the Commission as to AT & T's personnel
policies. Certain of these interrogatories are on a company-wide basis
while others asked for information on Bell System employment in 30
selected Standard Metropolitan Statistical Areas.

(2) Estimated Volume:

60 cubic feet.

(3) Finding Aids:

The exhibits and documents submitted in evidence are arranged in several
alpha-numeric series and a list of all of them is encluded.

(4) Interspersion of Valueless Material:

Small. There are a few duplicate copies of briefs and legal decisions
and some miscellaneous telephone company pamphlets and publications
which could be destroyed. The agency has already eliminated most of the
duplicates formerly present.

(5) Condition:

Very Good.

An appraisal report on accessioning National Archives records. (Records Disposition Division, National Archives)

(6) Frequency and Nature of Use:

Further use by the agency of origin is not expected. The records should be used several times a year by social historians and sociologists; business historians; and researchers in such fields as ethnic studies and the women's rights movement. There may be a possibility of use by other Government agencies and business firms with similar concerns.

(7) Restrictions on Use:

No specific restrictions. Records relating to charges of discrimination by specific individuals which were considered by EEOC, and which became part of these files because of their relevancy to the AT & T case, would presumably be covered by the National Archives general restriction on investigative records produced by executive agencies.

(8) Evaluation:

As indicated above, these records relate to legal proceedings of a very significant nature. The American Telephone and Telegraph Company and its associated Bell System companies comprise one of the largest privately owned organizations in the world--a regulated communications monopoly owned by more than three million shareholders and employing over 700,000 people. The proceedings by the Equal Employment Opportunity Commission, which charged the Bell companies before the regulatory Federal Communications Commission, with a pattern of discrimination in employment policies against minority groups and women extended for more than two years. The transcript of proceedings amounts to more than 7,000 pages. The size and scope of the final settlement bear out the significance of this litigation. These records, produced and collected by the "AT & T Task Force" of EEOC staff members, have a wealth of material on employment patterns throughout the country by an institution whose size and significance make it almost unique in the private sector. This litigation will inevitably be of great importance in the continuing development of employment discrimination law, particularly the interpretation of Title VII of the Civil Rights Act of 1964, the statute which created the EEOC. Although the records are naturally "advocate oriented" in reflecting EEOC's side of the argument, this is inevitable and can be allowed for. It should be noted that correspondence and interoffice memoranda relating to this litigation are still considered current records by the agency and are retained by it, particularly in the office of David Copus, the attorney in the Office of General Counsel who was in charge of handling the case for the Commission.

(9) Recommendation:

It is recommended that these records be accessioned by the National Archives.

Appraiser: _Charles South_ Date: 3/11/74

Appraisal Recommended: _Leonard Rapport_ Date: 3/12/74

In executing these plans, records administrators and archivists were faced with a basic question: What records are sufficiently valuable to merit permanent preservation? By 1945 the National Archives had begun to stress that the answer to this question, in broad terms, lies in identifying records that document significant administrative features of an agency and those that contain significant data relating to persons and things with which an agency dealt. A decade later this approach to selecting federal records for preservation received detailed treatment and official and professional sanction in writings of T.R. Schellenberg, who had become director of Archival Management at the National Archives, after having gained major experience in both historical research and archival administration. The research and administrative values of records, Dr. Schellenberg observed, are not necessarily mutually exclusive. "A record," he noted, "may be useful for various reasons." Usefulness for research, however, tends to be a predominant characteristic of the greater proportion of modern public records preserved in an archival institution.[3] Judging the research value of records is the most difficult and challenging task of an archivist. In this connection, a distinguished Canadian archivist has stated:

> The archivist . . . is called upon . . . to practice the difficult art of prophecy. He must attempt to anticipate needs. Out of a vast mass of material, a high percentage of which must be destroyed, he must try to identify and retain those items that are most likely to be of interest and significance in the years to come. Unlike the historian, the archivist cannot place any convenient subjective limitations on his field of interest. Somehow or other he must find means to pass judgment on the probable value of source material that may relate to virtually any aspect or period of the history of the state or country with which his institution happens to be concerned.[4]

What criteria then can the archivist use for selecting records? There are no precise criteria that can be applied in every situation. Experience, however, has provided some useful examples and guidelines for most situations. To begin with, there are well-known categories of records, long established through use as valuable research sources, that contain unique data on the nation's inhabitants. They include schedules of population censuses, military and naval service files, records relating to pensions for the armed services, case files of federal courts, and petitions and memorials from citizens. Such records are easily identified and readily enter the archival preserve.

Also readily identified for archival retention are those familiar groups of records that contain significant information about the nation's environment. Among these are weather reports, topographic maps, public construction case files, and descriptive records of basic natural resources. Moreover, there are records that regularly yield important information concerning national and possibly foreign activities and interests. The archival value of such materials is often immediately clear, as in the case of congressional proceedings, diplomatic correspondence and reports, patent case files, ship logs, and comprehensive statistical compilations and narrative reports on varied social, economic, and demographic trends.

These three broad types of records concerning individual experience, environmental history, and varied trends tend to be recurrent and yield fairly predictable types of data. There are many other kinds of records, however, that are not recurrent and must be closely analyzed to determine their value. In such an analysis, research value is considered to rest on a number of factors. To begin with, an effort is made to ascertain thoroughly the subject matter of the records in question. The uniqueness of the subject matter in light of all known published and unpublished documentation is then assessed. In the analysis process, the archivist uses his knowledge of historical writings and trends in historical research and his familiarity with related documents preserved in federal archives and other institutions. In dealing with highly specialized subjects, he may find it desirable to consult specialists in agencies that created the records or scholars who have done research on the subjects. His appraisal also involves consideration of the records' usefulness. Here he is concerned with physical characteristics that may affect usefulness and with estimates of the frequency and nature of use. As the agent of a public institution, a federal archivist retains records that will provide the greatest good for the greatest number of citizens. This tends to result in highest priority being given to preserving records of potentially varied research value, whose use seems likely to be sought by the greatest number of researchers and appear most likely to yield the greatest public benefit.

There are many examples of federal records in the National Archives Building relating to black Americans that illustrate the retention of records for research purposes. When this edifice was ready to receive the first records in 1935, it had been determined that there were in scattered government buildings vast and varied quantities of official papers. From this accumulation, federal archivists during the next decade selected several groups of records containing significant data on the black experience in America as well as other aspects of the nation's history. A few of these groups of records have an unusual concentration of data relating to major phases of the black experience. Especially noteworthy among these are records of the Bureau of Refugees, Freedmen, and Abandoned Lands, of black troops during the Civil War and later years, and of military commands governing southern states during the postwar period. The value of these documents is evident in numerous published and unpublished studies of recent years. Among these early accessions there are also varied and voluminous records often without a large concentration of data about blacks but which frequently include countless scattered files and individual papers relating to the black experience. Typical of these are records of Congress and the federal courts which illuminate more than a century of deliberations that concerned the fate of black Americans.

Other records accessioned early include the familiar statistical and biographical source materials that contain data on all segments of the American population. Illustrative of this category are schedules of population censuses, military service files, and pension records. Also documented in some of the earliest acquisitions are the experiences of blacks who lived outside the continental United States, as shown in records of Caribbean areas administered by the U.S. government and communications of foreign service posts in such countries as Africa and Latin America.

Since the 1940s, the legislation and regulations governing the archives have provided a basis for more systematic retention of federal records for research. The preservation of materials useful for black studies as well as for numerous other subjects has benefited accordingly. This growth in research resources coincided with the epochal growth of the federal government's concern with economic and social conditions during the 1930s. The government's increased interest in these conditions during the New Deal period produced large groups of records relating to activities which affected black inhabitants. The documentation of these activities, represented for example by records of the Works Progress Administration and National Recovery Administration and other agencies of the New Deal years, is vital for a thorough study of the black experience during the 1930s.

Similarly, in subsequent years government programs that have addressed problems of unemployment, health, and other socioeconomic matters, which have touched large groups of disadvantaged black Americans, have expanded. As these federal programs have expanded, in recognition of the irrepressible demands of the civil rights revolution, facilities for preserving an increasing volume of federal records relating to these developments have also grown. Archival facilities which house these records now include not only the National Archives Building but also archives branches in eleven federal records centers, and in some instances the six presidential libraries. Normally, valuable records of the headquarters of federal agencies are preserved in Washington; those of field offices are retained by the regional archives branches.

The vast stores of documents in these repositories offer unprecedented opportunities for research concerning black Americans. It is well to recognize, however, that the most profitable use of these resources for such research requires insight, ingenuity, and industry. Researchers in this field will find that the materials they seek are seldom segregated in large accumulations from other materials in the 456 record groups in the national archival system. Accordingly, they should have some knowledge of the government concern or contact that might have created the records being sought and should be prepared to make intensive searches in scattered parts of record groups. In such explorations, precise information concerning relevant persons, organizations, places, issues, and events is most productive. Students of black history, moreover, might well keep in mind that much of the black American experience, like that of the rustic Englishmen of Thomas Gray's elegy, is recorded in what he called the "short and simple annals of the poor." For many blacks, the words of Gray echoing across the centuries have a familiar relevance:

> . . . Knowledge to their eyes her ample page
> Rich with the spoils of time did ne'er unroll;
> Chill Penury repressed their noble rage
> And froze the genial current of the soul.

In the same way, the annals of black Americans have often been the creation of other persons. Hence, their experiences sometimes appear sporadically and incidentally in legislative records, judicial proceedings, executive correspondence, petitions and memorials of friends and enemies, and accounts of innumerable work projects that exacted their sweat and tears.

In summary it can be stated that federal records that enter the archival preserve deal with the experiences and the environment of all Americans. The experiences and environment of a particular segment of the American population may in a few instances be revealed in separate groups of records, but they are more likely to appear in numerous groups of records without racial categories or designations. A basic key to the identification of federal archives concerning black Americans or any other population group is both knowledge of federal policies, programs, and practices affecting that group and familiarity with federal agencies charged with developing and implementing such policy. Possession of such knowledge should greatly aid researchers who wish to discover more of the facts now so stridently demanded for the reappraisal of the black American heritage.

It is interesting to note that an important beginning of this reappraisal was undertaken nearly a century ago by George W. Williams, a black historian who examined documents of several American repositories and the British Public Record Office. In his *History of the Negro Race in America,* originally published in 1883 and now considered by many to be a landmark in American historiography, Williams stated an objective which researchers today might well follow as a guiding star. Commendably, he declared that his objective was to write "not as the blind panegyrist" of his race, "nor as the partisan apologist" but as one who writes "from a love for 'the truth of history.' "[5]

NOTES

1. U.S. American Historical Association, *Annual Report of the American Historical Association for the Year 1910* (Washington: Government Printing Office, 1912).
2. Address of Cordell Hull at the second meeting of the National Archives Council, 10 February 1936, *Second Annual Report of the Archivist of the United States,* pp. 4-5, National Archives and Records Service.
3. T.R. Schellenberg, *The Appraisal of Modern Public Records,* National Archives Bulletin no. 8 (Washington: National Archives and Records Service, 1956), pp. 7, 23.
4. W. Kaye Lamb, "The Archivist and Historian," *American Historical Review* 68 (January 1963): 385-86.
5. George W. Williams, *History of the Negro Race in America, 1619-1880* (New York: G.P. Putnam's Sons, 1968), p. 10.

Using Federal Archives: Some Problems in Doing Research

OKON EDET UYA

In his widely read book, *Creative History,* Walter T.K. Nugent remarked that historians "could no more function without libraries than chemists could function without Bunsen burners, zoologists without microscopes, or nuclear physicists without nuclear accelerators."[1] This comment is certainly applicable to archives, because here are found the historian's most important hardware: manuscripts. Although it is becoming increasingly fashionable, in this period of anti-intellectualism, to write history books without any significant archival research, it is still true that no monograph of significant depth and sophistication can be written without the long, tedious, often boring and unexciting exercise that archival research involves.

What is true of history in general is certainly true of that often neglected and distorted segment of the American experience—Afro-American history. In the current reappraisal of that experience, it is becoming obvious that to get away from this principle is to substitute passionate rhetoric for careful analysis and journalistic flair for fidelity to facts. Certainly, our goddess, Clio, is more exacting and demanding than that, and while we may, from time to time, wish to voice our own opinions we must recognize that we have to do so within the constraints established by this jealous muse. If Afro-American history is to achieve the prominence and academic respectability that it rightly deserves, we, its practitioners, must approach it with the seriousness of purpose and intellectual honesty demanded by our profession. To do less is to adumbrate the already too popular fallacy of black inferiority in yet another theater.

Archives and Historical Documents

History as we know or read it is basically a reconstruction of events based on a synthesis of fragments of evidences that testify to these events, which generally occurred in the past.[2] These "evidences," or documents, are the backbone of historical reconstruction. Depending on the cultural orientation of the groups involved and their level of technology, these evidences may be written (manuscripts, pictures, filmstrips, etc.) or oral (songs, folktales, proverbs, lists, epics, and other verbal testimonies generally described under the rubric of oral traditions).[3] The best-known depository of written documents is the federal archives.

The National Archives, the subject of our immediate concern, houses several pieces of information that are fundamental to our reconstruction of the Afro-American past. As indicated in *Black Studies: A Select Catalog of National Archives and Records Service Microfilm Publications,*[4] such information can be found in the records of the United States District Courts for the District of Columbia[5] covering the period from 1851 to 1863, which contain emancipation, manumission, and case papers concerning fugitive slaves.

The records of the Board of Commissioners for the Emancipation of Slaves contain minutes of board meetings, petitions that give the names of petitioners and slaves and their "monetary" value, as well as the action taken by the board on each petition.[6] The General Records of the Department of State (Record Group 59) contain papers detailing the activities of such black diplomats as Ebenezer D. Bassett, John Mercer Langston, Frederick Douglass, J. Milton Turner, Henry Highland Garnet, O.L.W. Smith, Ernest Lyon, R.T. Greener, William J. Yerby, James G. Carter, James Robert Spurgeon, Dr. George H. Jackson, and Herbert Wright, among others. Records of the Office of the Comptroller of the Currency contain signatures and personal identification data, which cover the period 1865-1874, about depositors in the twenty-nine branches of the Freedmen's Savings and Trust Company. Apart from the name of the depositor, account number, and date of deposit, these records provide such vital information as place of birth, place of residence, age, complexion, occupation, names of members of the family, data which, if used imaginatively, can provide invaluable information on Afro-American social history. The records of volunteer Union soldiers who served during the Civil War[7] are too familiar to merit elaborate attention here. Equally familiar and extensively used are the Freedmen's Bureau Records,[8] which give graphic descriptions of the heroic efforts to provide land, education, and other essentials which were needed to help the freed people bridge the gap from slavery to freedom. These records constitute a rather small sample of the variety of documents housed in the archives that relate to Afro-American history.

Nature of the Documents

For purposes of analysis, these documents can be divided into three groups: (1) those that describe the often conflicting and often vacillating, sometimes extremely confusing efforts of federal, state, and local governments and related agencies on behalf of blacks who were slaves, freedmen or victims of segregation and discrimination; (2) those that describe the activities of private philanthropic organizations that aimed their activities in the same general direction as government agencies; and (3) those that deal with the activities of blacks themselves either in their own behalf or in the service of the various agencies of the government.

The bulk of the records fall into the first two categories, and the following observations can be made about them. First, they describe the Afro-American experience from the outside in rather than from the inside out. This may lead, and in fact, has led to a situation where Afro-American history, for some, is nothing more than the sum total of the conflicting activities of the various government levels for or against black people. Such a history does no more than describe official governmental policies and cannot provide information on the internal dynamics of the Afro-American society. Second, especially in the case of the records of philanthropic organizations, the distress and misery of the target society is often, and quite understandably, overstated to justify the liberal posture of helping. In a case in 1865, for example, when agents of the Freedman's Bureau and philanthropic organizations described the freedmen of Port Royal in the Sea Island areas as ''a people scarcely emerged from childhood, an unfortunate class of people in such a state of abject ignorance and mental stolidity as to preclude any possibility of self-government and self-maintenance in their present condition,'' we clearly have zeal substituted for objective evaluation in the interest of philanthropy.[9] Overdependence on such sources has led to the pervasive pathological image of the Afro-

American experience in the historical literature.[10] Third, more often than not these records describe the black experience at moments of crises when that experience conflicts with the national posture: emancipation vs. slavery, integration and justice vs. segregation and discrimination. Given this orientation, such records focus very little attention on institutional continuities in the Afro-American communities, such as the family. Last, unless used with extreme care, these records can lead to the view that the Afro-American historical experience can be properly understood within the "white filter," the assumption being, as I have explained previously, that the general limits of the black experience can be understood by an analysis of certain pervasive white cultural and institutional mechanisms, operative at a given time, of which the black experience is merely a function.[11] As indicated earlier, this assumption has led to the view that the Afro-American historical experience can be properly understood as a function of governmental public policies, a contention that is coming increasingly under attack.

The third group of records, which deal with the activities of blacks themselves, presents a different set of problems. First, there are obvious gaps in the information which may present problems to the researcher. Not all the information solicited by the Freedmen's Savings and Trust Company, for example, with regard to age, residence, complexion, name of employer, occupation, place of birth, wife or husband, children, father, mother, brothers, sisters, remarks, and signatures was provided. Although the registers have been arranged alphabetically by state, city, date, and account number, many numbers are missing; a few are out of numerical order. Perhaps more serious is the problem associated with names. In the service records of volunteer Union soldiers, for example, the correct name of a soldier may not appear in the federal index because he may have served in a state unit or he may have served under a different name or a different spelling of his name. These discrepancies do present problems and can lead to distortions of historical facts. For example, Charlotte L. Forten in the *Journal of Charlotte Forten,* edited by Roy Allen Billington, describes an encounter between Thomas Higginson and one "Rob Small."

> Today Rob came to see me. I asked him how he was getting on in the store which he is keeping for the freedpeople. He said he was doing very well—making fifty dollars a week, sometimes. 'But,' said he, 'Gen. I'm going to stop keeping store. I'm going to enlist.'
> 'What,' said I, 'Are you going to enlist when you can make fifty doll[ar]s a week keeping store?' 'Yes, Sir,' he replied, 'I'm going to enlist as a private in the black regiment. How can I expect to keep my freedom if I'm not willing to fight for it? . . .'[12]

Robert Smalls (RG 200, Gift Collection, no. 64-M-190)

In his edited version, Billington makes the Rob Small of this encounter the Robert Smalls of the *Planter* fame, who subsequently fought in the Union navy. As I have indicated in my study of Robert Smalls,[13] although it is true that it was not until after the Civil War that he added the "s" to his last name, at no time did he keep a store in Beaufort.

Apart from names, there are other problems with the military records: an improper record of a soldier's service; possible destruction of records in the confusion that often attended initial mobilization, military operations, and disbandment of troops. A much more serious problem with military records is that although they provide information on an important segment of the black population, they tell us very little about the texture of life in the black community.

Limitations of Archival Research in Afro-American History

The problems outlined previously are not peculiar to archival materials dealing with the Afro-American past. By its very nature, archival material, though certainly the backbone of historical reconstruction, has several limitations. As indicated earlier, archives collect and keep, for the most part, written documents, but historical evidences can also be handed down orally. In fact, where the cultural orientation of the people is oral as opposed to written, as is certainly the case with the Afro-American, the most significant documents on the internal dynamics of that society and its cosmological orientation are bound to be oral rather than written. This merely restates a simple yet often forgotten problem of historians: the manner of preservation of historical facts is a function of the cultural orientation of the people. If we admit, as we increasingly appear to be doing, that Afro-American cultural orientation is more oral than written, that in the Afro-American community an individual of words and style is more likely to be heard than one of letters, although a combination of both is certainly an advantage, then we have to face the fact that the most significant documentation of Afro-American life is oral rather than written.

It is encouraging to note that historians of slavery, in varying degrees, are beginning to accept the fact that the slave songs and folktales, as well as the eyewitness accounts collected by the Works Progress Administration (WPA) in the 1930s are a much more valuable commentary on the slave's view of his condition than the records of the planters, their agents, sympathizers, and intellectual descendants.[14] Afro-American historians and researchers, therefore, can no longer ignore oral history as a fundamental adjunct to archival research in the reconstruction of the Afro-American past.

Oral Evidences: Their Nature and Uses

Oral history has many ramifications which cannot be discussed in this brief paper. For our purposes, I will limit the discussion to two kinds of oral evidences—oral traditions and eyewitness accounts.

Oral Traditions

Oral traditions, according to Jan Vansina, the best-known authority on the subject, are "verbal testimonies which are reported statements concerning the past."[15] Three points need to be emphasized about this definition. First, oral traditions are verbal, that is, handed down by word of mouth, and can therefore be sung or spoken (folktales, songs, proverbs, etc.). Second, since they are reported statements, the informant (interviewee) did not observe the event (referent) of which he speaks. Third, they concern the past and do not deal with the contemporary scene. Oral traditions, then, are part of the ethnographic data that comment on the past as perceived and conceived by the people and share three significant characteristics with other ethnographic data:

1. They are timeless, the only time expressed being the ethnographic present of the description. A Negro spiritual, for example, does not tell us when it began and continues to be relevant for our own generation;

2. They are situational, i.e., they testify to an event rather than give evidence about an event. In the folktales of the slaves, for example, we are given graphic illustrations of how old John and Br'er Rabbit manage to outwit the purportedly wise master and relatively stronger animal (Br'er Bear) without any explanation of the reasons for these dramatic triumphs; and,

3. Very importantly, they are practical and have immediate use and are therefore not subject to the embellishments and distortions of written records. When oral traditions no longer serve a useful purpose, they are promptly discarded. Their continued existence is therefore proof of their genuineness and importance in the cultural complex in which they exist.[16]

Oral traditions cover all aspects of society and culture. Although they may not provide quantifiable data, they provide information on all facets of material culture—art, demography, population movements, and religious and cosmological orientation. As I have explained previously,[17] slave songs, which are becoming increasingly widely accepted, comment not only on social relations within the slave community, but also, perhaps more importantly, on the religious and cosmological orientation of the slaves. A careful analysis employing the comparative culture analysis technique shows that slave songs are a significant commentary on the acculturation process during slavery.

One group of oral evidences that has to be increasingly utilized by Afro-American historians is the proverb. It must be borne in mind that in order to be popular to the people, a proverb must be adopted by the people to the extent that it becomes a summation of what they think is true. According to Kenneth Burke:

> Proverbs are strategies for dealing with situations. In so far as situations are typical and recurrent in a given social structure, people develop names for handling them.[18]

Consequently, whenever we use a proverb, we are invoking the experience of the group. In one sense, proverbs are group testimonies to the experiences of the group. For those interested in studying the interactions within the Afro-American family, it cannot be overemphasized that proverbs are very important commentaries on the socialization process in the community. Apart from being used to impart lessons in honesty and acceptable societal behavior, the rules governing the use of proverbs provide significant information on the concepts of responsibility, respect, and obligations in the community. Also, it is significant to note that proverbs are important rhetorical devices that may become decisive in verbal dueling and are, therefore, a fundamental part of the conception of leadership within the group. The point is that Afro-American historians ignore these oral historical evidences at their own peril.

Eyewitness Accounts

The second type of oral evidence that historians should use more is the eyewitness account. These are "documents" collected from people who observed or participated in the historical process described. Rather well-known examples are the slave autobiographies which John Blassingame, in his book, *The Slave Community,* has aptly described as "windows to the larger world of the plantation."[19]

The collection of eyewitness accounts, however, requires attention to specific techniques and details. Apart from the obvious problem of choosing the informant (interviewee), who must have been a "critical personality" in the events he describes, the collector must be familiar with all the elements that affect communication—the media, the goal, the site, the mood as conditioned by time, season, position of the informant, and duration, possible reactions and feedback and, most significantly, language.[20]

In using eyewitness accounts for historical reconstruction, the following points must also be kept in mind. First, the eyewitness is describing the events from a personal vantage point and may not be able to provide a total picture of the events that are discussed. In this case, the researcher must collect as many variants of the story as possible. Second, eyewitness accounts notoriously lack an account of what happened before and after the events described. Third, if the eyewitness is a stranger to the society he described (travelers, missionaries, etc.), he or she may not be able to place the event in the larger cultural context, and the real significance may thus be missed. Last, there is the human tendency for the eyewitness to exaggerate his importance in the events he described.

Despite these limitations, however, the systematic collection of eyewitness accounts by trained people must be embarked upon immediately. The Columbia Oral History Project has demonstrated the potential contribution of this area of research to American history generally. Certainly, as has been demonstrated by Raymond Wolters in his *Negroes and the Great Depression,*[21] there are a number of people able and willing to recapture graphically their experiences in the early decades of this century.

In conclusion, the reconstruction of an acceptable and meaningful Afro-American past where blacks are seen as more than mere victims of white oppression or as objects of white public and private sympathy requires that we use archival resources exhaustively but carefully. Also, it must be recognized that the very nature of the Afro-American historical experience—the often interrupted exclusion from full participation in mainstream American life, the African cultural pull, the oral cultural orientation—poses special problems for researchers in this field. A firm knowledge of Afro-American anthropology and sociology, as well as an acquaintance with the techniques of oral history, is essential for research in Afro-American history. Oral history is no substitute for archival research, but given the nature of Afro-American history, both will have to be used. Several libraries and state archives have, in fact, recognized this, and are taking an active role in the collection, processing, and preservation of oral materials. Perhaps participants of this conference should use this forum to appeal to the administrators of the National Archives to take a much more active role in the systematic collection of oral materials now underway. This is certainly consistent with the responsibilities it has accepted to encourage research and writing on the Afro-American past. Let us not forget Berkhofer's admonition that "only by exploring new forms of exposition can the historian write history complex enough to satisfy the dual goal of accurately analyzing the past and producing a work appealing to the complicated consciousness of the modern reader."[22]

NOTES

1. Walter T.K. Nugent, *Creative History* (Philadelphia: J.B. Lippincott, 1973), p. 27.
2. For a fascinating discussion of this process, see Robert Berkhofer, *A Behavioral Approach to Historical Analysis* (New York: Free Press, 1969), pp. 7-26.
3. For a classic discussion of the significance of oral traditions in historical reconstruction, see Jan Vansina, *Oral Traditions: A Study in Historical Methodology* (London: Routledge & Kegan Paul, 1965).
4. Stephen E. Hannestad and Claudine J. Weiher, comp., *Black Studies: A Select Catalog of National Archives and Records Service Microfilm Publications* (Washington, D.C.: General Services Administration, 1973).
5. Records of District Courts of the United States, Record Group 21, National Archives Building, Washington, D.C. These records have been microfilmed and are available as Microfilm Publication M433, 3 rolls.
6. Records of the United States General Accounting Office, Record Group 217, National Archives Building; Records of the Board of Commissioners for the Emancipation of Slaves in the District of Columbia, 1862-63, National Archives Microfilm Publication M520, 6 rolls.
7. Records of the Adjutant General's Office, 1780-1917, Record Group 94, National Archives Building; Microfilm Publication M589, 98 rolls.
8. Records of the Bureau of Refugees, Freedmen, and Abandoned Lands, Record Group 105, National Archives Building.
9. Cited in Thomas D. Howard, "The Freedmen's Paradise," *Charleston News and Courier*, 26 December 1888.
10. For an analysis of this view of Afro-American history, see S.D. Cook, "The Tragic Conception of Negro History," *Journal of Negro History* 50 (1965): 70-77.
11. Okon E. Uya, "Culture of Slavery: Black Experience Through a White Filter," *Afro-American Studies* 1 (1971): 203-9.
12. Ray Allen Billington, ed., *Journal of Charlotte Forten* (New York: Collier Books, 1961), p. 155.
13. *From Slavery to Public Service: Robert Smalls, 1839-1915* (New York: Oxford University Press, 1971).
14. Strangely enough, historian Eugene Genovese's book on slave religion draws extensively from the WPA collections in the Library of Congress and the Slave Collection at Fisk University.
15. Vansina, *Oral Traditions,* p. 19.
16. For a discussion of the uses of ethnographical data for historical reconstruction, see Vansina, "The Uses of Ethnographic Data as Sources for History," in *Emerging Themes of African History,* ed. T.O. Ranger (Nairobi: East Africa Publishing House, 1968), pp. 97-124.

17. Okon E. Uya, "The Mind of Slaves as Revealed in Their Songs," *A Current Bibliography on African Affairs,* 11th ser. 5 (1972); Sterling Stuckey, "Through the Prism of Folklore: The Blacks Ethos in Slavery," *Massachusetts Review* 9 (Summer 1968): 417-37.

18. Kenneth Burke, *The Philosophy of Literary Form* (New York: Oxford University Press, 1961), p. 256. See also Jack Daniels, "Towards an Ethnology of Afro-American Proverbial Usage," *Black Lines* 2, no. 4 (Summer 1972): pp. 3-12.

19. John Blassingame, *The Slave Community* (New York: Oxford University Press, 1972), p. 230.

20. For a full discussion of how these elements affect the collection of oral historical materials, see Leonard W. Doob, *Communications in Africa* (New Haven: Yale University Press, 1961), p. 15.

21. Raymond Wolters, *Negroes and the Great Depression* (Westport, Conn: Greenwood Press, 1970), p. 17.

22. Berkhofer, *Historical Analysis,* p. 321.

Discussion Summary

John H. Harmon, executive director of the Afro-American Cultural Foundation, observed that access to black folklore is fundamental to recording the history of Afro-Americans. He said that he had worked in Texas in 1935 on a Federal Writers Project and collected, edited, and published folklore materials on free Negroes and black cowboys. Harmon said that some of the data were not published because some found it unacceptable. He asked if those raw materials were now available.

In response, Harold T. Pinkett of the National Archives and Records Service stated that the records of the activities of the Works Progress Administration (WPA) headquarters are in the National Archives, and that these records contain a great deal of information concerning projects that were undertaken in several states. He added that much of the so-called source materials and background records that were actually created were not transferred to the National Archives at the time of the liquidation of the WPA. They were, if preserved at all, left in major repositories in the states. The University of Texas, for example, might have WPA source materials for that state. Pinkett then noted that the National Archives contains the registration of various state projects in headquarter records that were accumulated by the WPA.

Calvin M. Miller, chairperson of the Department of Political Science, Virginia State College, asked who had final authority over what documents would be archives and to what extent cultural and ethnic groups are represented in decisions regarding the retention of records.

Responding again, Pinkett held that under federal legislation, the preservation of records rests with the administrator of the General Services Administration, which is the parent organization of the National Archives and Records Service. The administrator delegates this responsibility to the archivist of the United States. Pinkett noted further that the archivist of the

Sign On | Basket

Search AbeBooks

Afro-american History by Clarke (8 results)

You searched for: **Author:** Clarke , **Title:** Afro-American History › *Edit your search*

Product Type

All Product Types
Books (8)

Search within these results

8 results

Sort By   Lowest Total Price   ▾   ▾ List   Grid

Magazines & Periodicals
Comics
Sheet Music
Art, Prints & Posters
Photographs
Maps
Manuscripts &
Paper Collectibles

Condition

All Conditions
New
Used

Stock Image

Book

Afro-American History: Resources for Research (National Archives Conferences, no. 12)

Clarke, Robert L. (ed.)

Published by Howard University Press, Washington, D. C., 1981

ISBN 10: 0882580183 ISBN 13: 9780882580180

Seller: Persephone's Books, Gastonia, NC, U.S.A.

Contact seller

Seller Rating: ★★★★★

Used – Hardcover
Condition: Very Good

US$ 25.00
Convert currency

US$ 4.50 Shipping
Within U.S.A.

Quantity: 1

Cloth. Condition: Very Good. No Jacket. xviii, 236 pp. The lightest of rubbing to the cover edges. The binding is tight and square, and the text is clean.

Condition

All Conditions
New
Used

Binding

All Bindings

Hardcover

Softcover

Collectible Attributes

First Edition (1)

Signed

Dust Jacket (4)

Seller-Supplied Images (2)

Not Printed On Demand

Free Shipping

Free US Shipping (4)

Seller Location

Worldwide

All Countries

Seller Rating

All Sellers

and up (7)

and up (7)

(6)

Seller Image

Afro-American history; sources for research

Clarke, Robert L.

Published by Howard University Press, Washington, 1981

ISBN 10: 0882580183 ISBN 13: 9780882580180

Seller: Bolerium Books Inc., San Francisco, CA, U.S.A.

Contact seller

Association Member: ABAA, ILAB

Seller Rating: ★★★★★

Book

Hardcover. xviii, 236p., illus., chipped dj with faded spine panel. National archives conferences volume 12.

Used − Hardcover

US$ 32.50

Convert currency

Free shipping
Within U.S.A.

Quantity: 1

AFRO-AMERICAN HISTORY: SOURCES FOR RESEARCH

Clarke, Robert L. Edited By

Published by Howard University Press, Washington, DC, 1981

ISBN 10: 0882580183 ISBN 13: 9780882580180

Seller: Du Bois Book Center, Englewood, NJ, U.S.A.

Contact seller

Seller Rating: ★★

Book   First Edition

Used − Hardcover
Condition: Very Good+++

US$ 30.00

Convert currency

US$ 5.00 Shipping
Within U.S.A.

Quantity: 1

United States relies heavily on advice given to him by specialists in various subject areas. He emphasized that the recommendations are made by persons who are trained in historical research. These archivists are familiar with research trends, they know which records have been used for particular subjects in the past, and they are conversant with the present trends and what might be expected to be of interest in the future.

Martin P. Claussen of Historiconsultants commented on Gus Low's analysis of the *Journal of Negro History*. Low's remarks highlighted the last few years of the journal's history, but did not mention articles based on archival research that had appeared in the journal much earlier. Claussen emphasized that one of the first articles based on archival research to appear in the journal was written in 1937 by James R. Mock and Carl Lokke, both National Archives staff members. Their article was entitled: "Records in the National Archives Relating to Negroes."

Jeannie A. Clark of Howard University said that she had done research in the Yoruba language that had won the attention of Nigerian universities. She asked Okon Edet Uya of Howard University about Nigeria's plans to expand the oral tradition method of research.

Uya replied that Nigeria's national archives collects oral traditions, and that these traditions are preserved as part of the Nigerian people's history. He stressed the view that one could not adequately reconstruct the Afro-American experience, given the cultural imperative of that experience, without doing more of what the Nigerian government and other African governments are doing. Uya observed that institutions should collect and keep these records before the people disappear from the scene. He also noted, "The more one reads the materials being published, the more one has the feeling that this is excellent work, but something is missing somewhere."

William Holton of the Department of Agriculture Graduate School observed that the number of oral history programs undertaken by various institutions had increased. He noted that there are about twenty-two oral history projects around the country, including those that are sponsored by Columbia University and other institutions. Holton then asked if the National Archives conducts an oral history program.

Pinkett stated that the National Archives, for a number of years, has carried out a progressive oral history program, particularly for the presidential libraries. He further noted that there have been interviews conducted with hundreds of persons, literally, who were associated with the presidents whose papers are preserved in the presidential library system. The National Archives and Records Service—in that particular part of the program, the library system—has carried on quite extensive work in the oral history area. Pinkett further commented that the National Archives would accession oral history materials, if they were accumulated in any important government activity. The Audiovisual Division of the National Archives has collected a great deal of oral materials, which was produced as a consequence of regular government activity.

II

Using Archives as Sources for Afro-American Research: Some Personal Experiences

A Love-Hate Relationship with the National Archives

MARY FRANCES BERRY

In using its resources for every one of my research projects since 1960, I have developed a long-standing love-hate relationship with the National Archives. I find the resources I need in its collections, but I often despair at the procedures for gaining access to them, which often impose frustrating barriers to the completion of work.

I began working in the Archives when I was a master's degree student in Howard University's History Department. Professor Elsie M. Lewis suggested that I do a master's thesis on the Louisiana Native Guards, some of the Negro troops who fought in the Civil War. After I accepted Professor Lewis' suggestion, she took me on my first visit to the Archives. I discovered the manuscript census of the United States, which I have utilized over and over again. Using the manuscript census and the military records (Record Group 94) for the Civil War period, I eventually completed my research on the Louisiana Native Guards. I discovered that the Archives had a large volume of materials on the military adventures of blacks and the development of military policy during the Civil War. My work was naturally made easier because of the quantity of materials available for analysis. Somewhat later, I discovered while reading an article on quantitative history that in preparing the study of the Louisiana Native Guards, I had produced some low-level quantitative history. I had analyzed the Native Guards in terms of their occupations and reported some simple yet interesting observations concerning occupational distribution. For example, about 10 percent of the group were carpenters and 2 percent were bricklayers in addition to the large number of unskilled laborers. I had made an unknowing excursion into quantitative history.

I continued research in military history during the Civil War as I began my dissertation at the University of Michigan. I expanded some of the work I had done previously in military history and incorporated research on conscription, including the enactment of the first national conscription act in 1863. As I developed a thesis in constitutional history of the United States, I used a number of Senate and House records, which were available in the National Archives, as well as the military records.

While I was attending law school at the University of Michigan, I continued to be challenged by Professor Lewis' questions and suggestions. She suggested I might be interested in knowing something about law and policy concerning the suppression of rebellions. She also queried me about the legal basis for the suppression of black rebellions in American history in the period before the Civil War.

In order to answer her questions and to respond to her suggestion, I used the National Archives records once again. In addition to research in various law libraries, I came to the National Archives and began working in the Department of Justice records (Record Group 60.) I used the attorney general's and district attorney's records in the various states in the South in order to understand the development of the law, how it had been interpreted, and how it had been enforced in cases of black resistance. I expanded the study to include the period after the Civil War.

My third experience in using the National Archives came about in answer to a question I posed for myself. As I prepared lectures for my black history class, I noticed that in the period between the end of Reconstruction and about 1916, the usual topics of discussion in every study concerned Booker T. Washington, W.E.B. Du Bois, Henry M. Turner, the Afro-American League or Council, and the rise of the NAACP. Not much was included beyond these subjects. It occurred to me that I needed to know more about blacks beyond these very well-known figures in order to give students a more realistic picture of the times. Realizing as I did by that time that law is one of the most influential forces in the existence of human beings, a prism through which one can examine the human experience, I decided to look at some of the court cases to find out whether there had been some unnoted black people involved who had made significant contributions about which I could tell my students.

Portions of an official letter on the East Saint Louis race riots from Major R.W. Cavinaugh to the adjutant general of the United States Army. (RG 60, Department of Justice)

East St. Louis,Ill.,July 26,1917

From: C.O. Detachment 6th Reg., Ill. Inf.,NG.

To: Commanding General, Central Department, Chicago, Ill.

Subject; The situation at East St. Louis.

1. The situation for the last two or three weeks has been apparently normal excepting for the presence of the troops patroling the
streets and continually keeping the reason they are there for in the
minds of the people and seems to cause a feeling of unrest. There has
also been brought to our attention a great manny instances of laborers
such as icemen, deliverymen, etc., telling what they are going to do
to the negroes when the troops leave. There is no questionin my mind
but what these have been exaggerated.

2. As you know, there has been a great many investigation committee at work but so far as actual results being obtained they are exactly
where they started. In the beginning the men we took in as rioters that
night were let go the following morning, some with very small fines,
others on bail and others dismissed. This continued to be the program
of the men arrested by the military until such a time as General Dicken
and myself rose up and demanded that something else be do ne as the same
men we had arrested, as soon as they were free, were back on the job
again and the military were going around in a circle so far as doing
anything for the permanent peace.

3. It is now a little better as the Grand Jury is indicting some
and some have been sent to jail but only too few have had the fear of
God put into them therefore it continues disordered in the town.

4. Everybody seems to be passing the buck until it lands on the
police department which consists of only 69 men in all departments,
allowing 26 police for the day and 11 for night work. The mayor has the
resignation of the three police commissioners who it seems are the only
ones who have the power to reorganize the force and has appointed three
representatives men of good standing to take their places who admit
themselves that they will not even accept or make any plans until such
time as the various industries show them in the bank to their credit
$105,000 which it is claimed they will need to put the police depart-
ment in good condition and if the money is not fortncoming they say
they are through without even starting.

5. At a conference held with the Finance Committee and these
three commissioners, Wednesday, these facts were brought out, mind you
at this late date. The finance committee believe they will have the
money raised by Friday morning at which time they will hold another
meeting and the military will be informed of the findings.   It was
suggested that each firm could pick out as manny of their trusted
employees as they could and have them deputized by the mayor or sheriff
as deputy police and put to work in the vicinity of their plants.

Rec'd Central Dept. JUL 28 1917

Major 6th Ill. Inf.

1st Ind.   SCM

Hq. Central Dept., Chicago, Ill., July 29, 1917 - To The Adjutant General of the
army, ashington, D.C.   A copy of this letter has been sent to the Governor
of Illinois with request that he take steps to straighten out matters insofar
as the Municipal Government and especially the police department of East St.Louis
are concerned.

Major General.

Shown to the Secretary

The Adjutant General

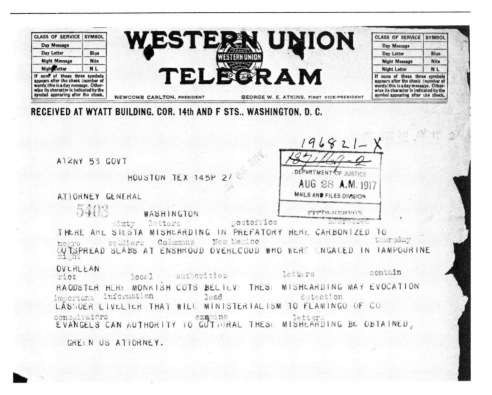

A Western Union telegram and special on the East Saint Louis race riots, August 28, 1917. (RG 60, Department of Justice)

As I searched records at the National Archives, I became aware of an organization called the Ex-Slave Pension and Bounty Movement. I discovered a woman called Callie House about whom I had known nothing, and I found that she was one of a number of black people who thought beyond forty acres and a mule as a viable economic solution during Reconstruction and thereafter. She believed that reparations paid to blacks by the government was a fair and equitable proposition. The district court records and the Bureau of Pension records in the Archives helped me to trace bills that she had had introduced in Congress to provide for reparations. I was also able to follow Callie House's career, as the Postal Department had her convicted for mail fraud and imprisoned. The government believed that, like Marcus Garvey later, she had defrauded members of her organization by accepting dues to support a movement for reparations which had no possibility for success and therefore was not a worthy enterprise.

370.61 E.St.Louis

WESTERN UNION SPECIAL

B 132 W.KE.   176 Blue   9 EX

St Louis Mo   July 3rd, 1917   756

Adj General

        War Dept Washington DC

EastLouis in hands of mob entirely beyond control the local
authorities and illinois state troops threats of burning and
destruction of leading manufacturing plants openly made including Aluminum Ore Co, Commercial Acid Co, Kehlor Flour
Mills, Corno Mills Co, General Roofing Mfg Co, Hammer White
Lead Company and others The destruction of any of these
plants in this will will be injurious to the interests of
the National government and in addition they have the right
to appeal for protection which is not given by any local
authorities reports indicate much worse action tonight than
last night immediate action necessary government troops at
these plants or in the city with proper instructions can
handle the situation immediately V A Layman chairman of our
committee is at NewWillard Hotel Washington I am sending
copy of this message to him but am telegraphing as vice chairman of this committee at special request of large business
interests which feel they can only look to you for protection
will you act immediately.

                Geo M Brown, Vice Chairman Advisory Committee
                    on Purchase of Army supplies

730PM

Tel Sent to CD Jul 5

A recent question I have asked myself which requires working again in the National Archives, involves the comparative effect of law enforcement in criminal cases concerning blacks and whites in particular jurisdictions throughout the country. We discuss police brutality and the oppressiveness of law enforcement as we analyze contemporary events, but police brutality has a history. I think we should determine how, in fact, criminal law was enforced against blacks and whites throughout American history in every local jurisdiction. To begin addressing that issue, one must search the court and Justice Department records which are collected in the National Archives.

Despite my frustrations at not being able always to gain direct access to records when I choose, I have found that the National Archives is the depository of valuable records which highlight the history of public policy toward blacks. For me, as for other historians, the exchange of ideas and information with the staff of the National Archives will undoubtedly be a lifetime experience.

Using Federal Archives for Research: An Archivist's Experience

ROLAND C. McCONNELL

In using federal archives, my involvement with the National Archives has been twofold: in an internal capacity as a regular staff member, and in an external relationship as a research scholar and college professor. These experiences have not only complemented each other but have become inextricably related in such a manner as to afford a most rewarding and enriching endeavor in research and scholarship that has continued to the present.

In 1943 I was assigned to the War Records Branch of the National Archives and soon thereafter was placed in charge of the Records of the Office of the Quartermaster General (Record Group 92). Four persons were assigned to me for the purpose of effectively servicing the records. In this branch, I learned the nature and function of federal archives and the skills that were necessary for archival work, which included preservation and care of records, including boxing, shelving, and filing; searching and answering requests and compiling reports; and analysis and description of records including the preparation of finding aids.

Each new search of archival records that I conducted increased my awareness of their significance. One example was my discovery of the "Report of Persons Employed and Articles Hired by the Quartermaster." In the column of the record entitled "by whom owned" appeared the word *contraband*.[1] This term helped to explain, in innumerable instances, the transitional phase of the black experience from slavery to freedom. This report also revealed how the black man and woman got into the war effort, while the question of utilization of black manpower in the military was being debated, long before the Emancipation Proclamation was issued.

In the quartermaster report, the names of both men and women appear on the rolls with their occupations, rates of pay, days worked, and other detailed items—all of which enhance the value of the records for research purposes.[2] The men usually worked as builders of fortifications and roads, and the women as cooks, nurses, and hospital aides.

Christopher Crittenden, director of the North Carolina State Department of Archives and History and editor of the *North Carolina Historical Review,* invited me to write the article "Records in the National Archives pertaining to the History of North Carolina." Preparation for this article, which involved searching the period between 1775 and 1943, gave me the opportunity to become acquainted with practically every record group in the National Archives. After a two-year working period, the research was completed and the article appeared in the July 1948 issue of the *North Carolina Historical Review.*[3]

Shortly after the paper on North Carolina appeared, I published an article entitled "Isaiah Dorman and the Custer Expedition" in the *Journal of Negro History,* July 1948.[4] This, I believe, was the first time attention was directed to the part played by a black man in connection with the Custer Expedition. As a result, the eminent Carter G. Woodson invited me to prepare a paper based on archives for the Annual Meeting of the Association for the Study of Negro Life and History, October 1949. The paper, entitled "Importance of Records in the National Archives on the History of the Negro," afforded me a second tour of record groups in the National Archives.[5] The format of the paper followed that of the one on North Carolina, except that it included additional information on the organization and usage of archives. In writing the article, I used *A Guide to Documents in the National Archives for Negro Studies* by Paul Lewinson.[6] This guide was a practical tool for searching the archival records. The paper was printed in the April 1949 issue of the *Journal of Negro History.*[7]

During my early years at Morgan State University, I had the privilege of processing the manuscript collection of Emmett J. Scott. The university had acquired the collection through its President, Dr. Martin D. Jenkins. Scott had served successively as assistant to the secretary of war; secretary-treasurer of Howard University; chairman, Negro Branch of the National Republican Party; and director of personnel, Shipyard Number 4, Sun Shipbuilding and Drydock Company, Chester, Pennsylvania. With the exception of the records of the secretary-treasurer, sizable record holdings for each of these offices were transferred to Morgan State University. The structure of these records lent itself to processing that involved several archival functions: survey and acquisition, boxing and shelving, analysis and description, and finally preparation of a checklist.[8]

Other collections were acquired and processed by Morgan State. Included were the papers of Judge Morris Soper, chairperson of the university's board of trustees, and the papers of D.O.W. Holmes, the first black president of Morgan State University. I was also commissioned to process the Holmes papers for the university.

The concept of college archives increasingly attracted me. Using the Morgan State experience as a prototype, I wrote an article, "The Small College and the Archival Record," which appeared in the *Journal of Negro Education* in the winter of 1963.[9] In the article, I suggested the possibilities of college archives and projected the realities of such a proposal based on my experience at Morgan State. Although the impact of this article is unknown elsewhere, the interest of Morgan State University in the acquisition of papers of prominent figures in and concerned with Afro-American experiences and treating them archivally, whenever possible, continues.

One of my experiences in working with archival materials was stimulated by the records of the War Office pertaining to personnel, which contain valuable information on blacks. This is especially true of the muster rolls of black soldiers in the United States Armed Services. Particularly challenging are the rolls of the Corps d'Afrique. Returning to the National Archives for subsequent work on this organization, I discovered that they were at one time known as Louisiana Native Guards and that their ancestors had fought during the war of 1812 in the Battle of New Orleans, under the command of Gen. Andrew Jackson. I immediately began to write an article entitled "Negro Soldier in the Battle of New Orleans" and to search the muster rolls involved.

Discovering after further survey that the Free Men of Color who engaged in the Battle of New Orleans constituted an entire regiment, I soon conceived the idea of writing a book instead of an article on Andrew Jackson and the Negro soldier. Further research into the records, especially the personnel records, revealed that the two battalions that composed the Afro-American regiment had important antecedents. The original battalion of Free Men of Color had a history that could be traced to the Spanish Regime in Louisiana. Moreover, a number of these soldiers had ancestors who served under the French in their wars against the Indians in the early eighteenth century. The idea now took hold to search for materials for a book on the black soldier. The idea became a reality with the publication of

Carded Civil War documents describing a black soldier's military career.
(RG 94, Adjutant General's Office)

the book in 1968, *Negro Troops of Antebellum Louisiana: A History of the Battalion of Free Men of Color.*[10] From the inception of the idea in 1948 to the completion of the work in 1968, I spent several years researching, including a sabbatical.

Although extensive research was conducted in New Orleans and at the Library of Congress, the records at the National Archives remained the major source of my information for this book. Especially significant and vital to the work were Records of the Veterans Administration (Record Group 15); Records of the Bureau of Land Management that contain an individual file for each veteran who applied for a disability benefit or bounty land, respectively, or both (Record Group 49); and Records of the Adjutant General's Office, which included the muster roll and payroll for each company of Free Men of Color (Record Group 94). Without researching these records, this particular book could not have been written.

Other record groups in the National Archives were helpful. Among them were General Records of the Department of State that include the thirteen volumes of original letters, documents, and other communications of W.C.C. Clairbone, the governor of New Orleans, to the secretary of state (The Clairbone Letter Books have been published) (Record Group 59); Records of the U.S. Army Commands, 1784-1821 (Record Group 98); and Records of the Office of the Secretary of War, containing correspondence from General Jackson and Governor Clairbone of Louisiana (Record Group 107).

In writing the book, *Negro Troops of Antebellum Louisiana: A History of the Battalion of Free Men of Color,* the records in the National Archives were by no means exhausted. Biographical sketches of a number of little known, but deserving personalities await research as well as the entire story of bounty land and black people.

While the writing of a book may have been the high point of my external archival relationship, as far as productivity is concerned, another dimension of my experience has been through my students. Two of these students immediately come to mind. At the inception of the Graduate School at Morgan State University, Charles Johnson used the records of the Department of the Army in writing his thesis, "The Tenth Cavalry (United States), 1866-1900." Kennard H. Wright used the records of the United States Maritime Commission in researching and writing his thesis, "American Negro Maritime War Effort, Sun Shipyard No. 4, 1942-45."

Thus my personal experiences and those of my students in using archives as sources have not only been fruitful but also continuous and ever enlightening.

NOTES

1. See "Report of Persons Employed and Articles Hired by the Quartermaster, U.S. Army," Records of the Office of the Quartermaster General, Record Group 92, National Archives Building, Washington, D.C.
2. Ibid.
3. Roland C. McConnell, "Records in the National Archives Pertaining to the History of North Carolina, 1775-1943," *North Carolina Historical Review* 25 (1948): 318-40.
4. Idem, "Isaiah Dorman and the Custer Expedition," *Journal of Negro History* 33 (1948): 344-52.
5. Idem, "Importance of Records in the National Archives on the History of the Negro," *Journal of Negro History* 34 (1949): 135-52.
6. Paul Lewinson, comp., *A Guide to Documents in the National Archives for Negro Studies* (Washington: American Council of Learned Societies Executive Offices, 1947), p. 3.
7. McConnell, "Importance of Records in the National Archives on the History of the Negro," pp. 135-52.
8. Idem, comp., "Preliminary Inventory of the Papers of Emmett J. Scott Collection in Morgan State College, 1916-1951," mimeographed (Baltimore: Morgan State College, Soper Library, 1959).
9. Idem, "A Small College and the Archival Record," *Journal of Negro Education* 32 (1963): 84-86.
10. Idem, *Negro Troops of Antebellum Louisiana: A History of the Battalion of Free Men of Color* (Baton Rouge: Louisiana State University Press, 1968), p. 1.

Federal Archives as a Source for Determining the Role of Mary McLeod Bethune in the National Youth Administration

ELAINE M. SMITH

When Mary McLeod Bethune arrived at the train station in Chicago one fall morning in 1937, such a flurry of activity swirled around her that one bystander asked, "Who is she?—a movie star?" Judging from the gala and sometimes tumultuous receptions people everywhere accorded this five feet-four inch stately matron, that question may have been asked more than once. But fortunately, Bethune was not a film titan but the towering black leader in the second quarter of this century. In the face of that era's legal racial segregation and discrimination, she struggled for black equality within the context of an ultimately integrated society and her widespread popularity indicates that she advanced this cause ably.

Though born in distressful circumstances in rural South Carolina in 1875, Bethune had sterling experiences in her first twenty-one years which paved the way to national prominence. She found a sense of security based upon faith in God and then in herself. She associated with two dynamic black women who had established schools. She received encouragement from them and others to express a deeply-rooted missionary inclination. She imbibed the character of an exemplary educational institution by attending one. And finally, she developed a cosmopolitan orientation in Chicago via contact with people from around the world.

Mary McLeod Bethune (RG 200, Gift Collection, no. 200(S)-HNP-6)

With this undergirding her life became a record of public service. In 1904, in Daytona Beach, Florida, she established an institution which grew into Bethune-Cookman College, the cornerstone of her career. During the 1920s she held the very prestigious position of president of the National

Association of Colored Women. In 1935 she began work on behalf of the federal government's National Youth Administration (NYA). This connection gave her leverage in creating two new race organizations: the National Council of Negro Women, to promote visibility for ebony women in public affairs; and the Federal Council on Negro Affairs, alias the "Black Cabinet," to facilitate the collective action of black government officials on pressing concerns of Afro-Americans. The NYA affiliation also provided Bethune with a convenient base for representing the Roosevelt administration to blacks and vice versa. Though her activities were wide-ranging in the late 1930s and early '40s, her priority work was within the NYA program.

By executive order under the Emergency Relief Appropriations Act, the NYA was created on June 16, 1935, for young people aged sixteen to twenty-four. Whether they were in or out of school, its chief objective was to put them to work during the Great Depression. Even when World War II spending revived the economy the NYA continued its service because many youth still needed assistance. The agency employed several million. For example in 1941, a boom year, with more than $157,000,000 it put roughly 750,000 young people to work.

Although the NYA enjoyed considerable autonomy in policy matters and retained the same administrator, during its nine year history it experienced important administrative changes. It was lodged successively in three larger organizations: the Works Progress Administration, the Federal Security Administration, and the War Manpower Commission. During the Depression its program was administered essentially through state directors wielding significant discretionary powers. But during the war, the program became regionally based.

In researching Mary Bethune's role in the NYA I used several primary sources to obtain data on the Negro program and on the framework in which it operated. I interviewed a few of Bethune's New Deal associates. I read newspapers and periodicals, particularly the *Pittsburgh Courier,* the weekly in which Bethune published a column in 1937 and '38. I visited the Bethune Foundation in Daytona Beach, the depository Bethune, herself, established. I discovered NYA materials there which duplicate those in the National Archives and others which are unavailable elsewhere, especially for the 1940s. And, of course, I perused National Archives records both at the Washington headquarters and the Franklin D. Roosevelt Library, a subdivision located in Hyde Park, New York. All of these sources yielded helpful data but the single most important one was the Archives.

At the Archives in Washington, the records of the National Youth

Administration are designated as Record Group 119. They comprise eleven hundred cubic feet. Of the nearly twenty major subdivisions of these records, understandably, the group created by the Office of Negro Affairs was the most helpful. These papers, however, are limited. Enclosed in fifteen document containers, they comprise only a few cubic feet, include solely the records of the director of the office and cover primarily the 1935-39 period. They constitute an assortment of materials: reports, proposals, correspondence, memoranda, applications for student aid, publications, newspaper clippings, bibliographies, and miscellaneous items. Of the files into which these Negro records are organized, the one labeled "File of Early 'Inactive' Correspondence" is the most concentrated single group of documents bearing upon Bethune's functioning within the NYA. The reports therein relate to the status of Negro activities which was assessed at different intervals, NYA Negro conferences, state advisory committees, and site visits.

Considering all the Office of Negro Affairs documents, perhaps three are illustrative of their character and value. First, the report of the Conference of Negro Activities, August 8, 1935, reveals Bethune's early inclination to aggressively represent the interests of Negro youth. Second, a Bethune confidential report of 1938 shows that, on occasion, she could bluntly state embarassing facts despite her penchant for bureaucratese (language frequently obscuring more than revealing). And third, the 1943 Final Report of the Negro Division brings to light a grand sweep of information including stellar projects designed for Negro youth.

Aside from the papers of the Negro Office, I found three other subdivisions of Record Group 119 particularly pertinent to my study. Records of the National Advisory Committee, the Thelma McKelvey File, indicate the attitudes of NYA executives relative to black participation and Bethune's presumptuous actions as an NYA adviser. The Records of the Office of the Administrator illuminate the early recognition of blacks within the program; the situation regarding the employment, activity, and resignation of Juanita Saddler, the first black NYA staff official; and the perception of Bethune's office as a forum for appeal among black staff members at the state and local levels.

The third subdivision, the NYA Publications File, which includes proceedings of several conferences, contains valuable data. Bethune was in evidence at three of these conferences. The first was the 1936 National Advisory Committee Meeting. The other two, in 1936 and 1939, were national forums which Bethune organized and chaired on the "Problem of the Negro and Negro Youth." The proceedings of meetings held in 1935 and 1936 for NYA State Youth directors were interesting not because Bethune was present or because they disclosed discussion of Negro involvement in NYA, but because there was a virtual absence of references to blacks, thus suggesting that although the agency could tout some black activity at the time, within the scope of its total program Afro-Americans were of minuscule concern.

Even though reading NYA documents was crucial to describing and assessing Bethune's work, my search in the National Archives in Washington was incomplete until I examined its audiovisual records. These include a 1943 seven-minute sound recording of Bethune's broadcast to the British West Indies supporting the allied war effort. Though obviously the address was tangent to the NYA, hearing Bethune's rich, resonant voice gives added dimensions to her speeches championing the youth agency. The audiovisual materials on the NYA Negro program consist of approximately three hundred pictures and two films. One of the films, ''Youth-Building at Wilberforce,'' shows Bethune approving that Ohio university's NYA project.

Turning to the Archives' presidential library at Hyde Park which houses the papers of President and Mrs. Roosevelt and those of many of their contemporaries and associates, I searched in four manuscript collections beginning with the president's. Though Roosevelt's Official and Personal Files contain Bethune letters, these did not highlight the black administrator's role within the NYA. Slightly better in this regard were the papers of Charles Taussig, the chairman of the NYA National Advisory Committee, and Aubrey Williams, the NYA administrator. Taussig's papers indicate Bethune's long-term input into the Advisory Committee. Williams' papers expose personnel matters relative to Bethune and the respect Williams had for her. Moreover, in light of the friendship between Mary Bethune and Eleanor Roosevelt, both these collections bear on the climate in which Bethune worked by pointing to the First Lady's god-motherly interest in the National Youth Administration and her close contact with its chiefs. In contrast to the other manuscript collections in the library, the papers of Eleanor Roosevelt contain voluminous Bethune correspondence. Although most of it does not deal specifically with the NYA, some such nuggets are strewn around. For example, one of them illustrates Bethune's dilemma of maintaining credibility both within the black population and the white hierarchy in the light of conflict on a given issue between those in the two camps.

When I considered data from the various records in the National Archives pertinent to Bethune's NYA career, especially in conjunction with records from other sources, the contours of her role within the agency were evident. She became affiliated with the Youth Program in August 1935 as one of the thirty-five members on its National Advisory Committee. Though the position primarily required attendance at annual or semi-annual meetings, Bethune worked for the program as if she were on the payroll. To give her latitude, the NYA hired her in June 1936 as an administrative assistant and in 1939 officially promoted her to director of the Division of Negro Affairs. As an NYA staff official, her role was similar to that of other blacks who worked in federal agencies as specialists on Negro problems during the New Deal. Coupling vigilance with moral suasion, she was to facilitate equitable benefits for blacks within the National Youth Administration. In the light of the racism rampant in American life and the character of the NYA administrative organization, this was a formidable job in which the goal of equality could not be realized especially in terms of proportionate expenditures for Negro youth vis-a-vis white. Nevertheless, Bethune made gallant efforts with substantive results. She was crucial in creating positions for black administrators in the NYA at the national, state, and regional levels and she assisted them when possible. She helped to broaden the base of black participation in each of the three major NYA program components: part-time employment for young people in school; work-relief and vocational training projects for those out of school; and placement service for those prepared to enter private industry. During the Depression Bethune was most successful in the school-aid program, in which she persuaded the agency to establish a special Negro fund in higher education. And during the war, within the context of industry's demand for trained labor, she realized basic objectives in the other two NYA program components.

During Bethune's NYA days, people across the land knew that she was doing a great work though they probably did not understand its ramifications. Today, through the National Archives' NYA records and its papers of New Deal public servants, one can enter the past documenting, sometimes precisely, things which an older generation intuitively sensed about Mary McLeod Bethune and the National Youth Administration. For this, and for the perspective on an era which the records provide, we can all be grateful.

Discussion Summary

The discussion was initiated by Rosalyn T. Penn of Morgan State University, who asked about the records pertaining to the suppression of rebellions in which blacks engaged prior to the Civil War.

Mary Frances Berry of the University of Maryland observed that the General Records of the Department of Justice, Record Group 60, contained a wide range of documents that outlined the provisions that were made to suppress rebellious and resistance activities in which blacks were engaged. She further replied that in her book *Black Resistance, White Law,* she discussed something she called legal racism. In researching the records, she had identified the constitutional provisions and the statutes that presidents of the United States and cabinet officials used to call out troops to suppress such activities.

As a result of her study, Berry discovered that one of the purposes of Article 4, Section 4 of the Constitution was to make sure that provisions would be made to suppress any kind of rebellion in which blacks were engaged. She also observed that this control was much more extensive than most people might have thought, since it was an apparatus of control by design—and a very effective one. The other value of the study, Berry noted, was in addressing the debate about whether slaves were docile or why blacks did not rebel.

Elaine M. Smith of Tuskegee Institute shared her findings in regard to Mary McLeod Bethune and the National Youth Administration (NYA). Penn asked Smith if she had found any information which defined Bethune's relationship to Lyndon Baines Johnson. Smith replied that she had researched part of the Records of the National Youth Administration (Record Group 119), and she noted that Johnson had worked in the NYA as the state director of the Texas program. She saw references to the Texas Youth Program, but could find no direct communication between the two.

Vincent Harding of the Institute of the Black World, Atlanta, Georgia, was concerned about the records that document the use of white law in dealing with the twentieth-century freedom movements. He asked how much material was available under the new declassification laws for the post-World War II period of FBI and military intelligence, especially files having to do with freedom movements in the United States.

Berry replied that in her own work, she found that declassification was a real problem. In a number of cases, she attempted to look at the material but was not able to do so, although she pleaded the Freedom of Information Act in several instances. She talked to Attorney General Richard G. Kleindienst and Justice William H. Rehnquist and others concerning the release of information. She also added that she has letters in her files in which certain officials explained why she could not see certain records, even though she knew that they were available and "the trails led to their door."

Leon F. Litwack of the University of California asked about the restrictions on investigative-type materials. He wondered whether there was a general rule of a seventy-five year restriction on access to such records.

A National Archives staff member responded that access to investigative records is restricted for seventy-five years. This material is available to an archivist only if the agency indicates that it has no further administrative use. The National Archives has accessioned only a small amount of material from the FBI, mainly because FBI holdings generally are considered to be of an investigative nature. These records are not accessible to researchers because the FBI was not established until 1908; therefore, the seventy-five year restriction period has not yet elapsed.

Litwack observed that the Department of Justice was active in investigating so-called subversive groups among blacks. For example, one can obtain a copy of the famous report that A. Mitchell Palmer issued entitled "Pro-Germanism among Negroes." Another report deals with seditious subversive organizations among blacks. Both reports were included in the investigative report of the Chicago 1919 riot.

In response to a question from the floor about the possibility of an individual bringing suit to obtain disclosure under the Freedom of Information Act, Berry answered that a number of people have brought suit under that act. She recalled that while she worked for a government agency, a number of people invoked the Freedom of Information Act in order to obtain records. In attempting to obtain these records, several people have been unsuccessful mainly because one section of that act excludes access to internal memorandums as well as other sensitive materials.

A commentator from the floor closed the discussion with the question: How valuable are police records in revealing facts about people that cannot be found as conveniently in other sources? Berry responded that researchers can find a wide range of useful materials in police records and other legal records, i.e., historical records that reflect "what people are doing and what is happening to them." Another commentator observed that in all situations where there is oppression or colonization, a major part of the history of the oppressed people would be found in the police records of the colonizers.

III

The
Multipurpose
Use of
Federal Archives

Boston, April 26. 1869.

To His Excellency
The President of the United States.
The undersigned, citizens of
Massachusetts, respectfully request that Mr. Frederick
Douglass of Rochester, New York, be appointed United
States Minister to Brazil.

[Two columns of signatures follow]

Robt C. Pitman
Julius A. Palmer
Edmund Dowse
F. A. Hobart
Geo. A. King
Chas. L. Ladd
Ester Cow
Joseph Tucker
Thos. Rice Jr.
M. Endicott
M. S. Underwood
Wm. Adams Jr.
Thos. Talbot.
A. Warner.
Jacob H. Loud
Henry B----
Theo. A. Cunningham
Nehemiah Brown
Henry Edwards
J. H. Piper
David Pulsifer
Lewis Hayden

J. F. Gifford
R. Kingman
Benj. C. Dean
John J. Baxter
E. S. Whittemore
Martin----
J. F. Swift
Henry B. Wheelwright
D. H. Rogers
George Phillen
Edmund Davis

E. Herbert Cliff
N. A. Kegan
A. S. Allen
W. W. Bullock
Chas. Millett
Leonard Vinson
Saml. P. Hack
E. P. Robinson
F. M. Chase.

A typical signature page of an appointment paper. (RG 56, Department of the Treasury)

Federal Appointment Papers and Black History

JAMES D. WALKER

The appointment of blacks to prominent positions in the federal government remains an undocumented area in American history. Who are they? When were they appointed? And where can one find information about their appointments?

We know today of those persons who achieved national prominence by their election to Congress and their services in high-level federal positions. Among them are Edward Brooke, Blanche K. Bruce, and Hiram Revels as U.S. senators; Shirley Chisholm, Charles C. Diggs, Jr., John A. Hyman, Barbara Jordan, John M. Langston, Adam Clayton Powell, and Josiah T. Walls as congresspersons; Ralph Bunche, William H. Hastie, and Emmett Scott as diplomats; George L.P. Weaver as assistant secretary of labor; and Robert Weaver as the first black cabinet member.

Other blacks who served in notable positions in the federal government were William D. Crum, Frederick Douglass, James T. Rapier, Harry Rucker, Robert Smalls, and Daniel Hale Williams. Many blacks remain unnamed, although they held responsible positions in the federal government.

The U.S. political system has means of reward and punishment. Sometimes local members of the various political parties contribute their time, efforts, and money to elect members of their parties to office. After an election, the successful candidates reward some faithful supporters by appointing them to positions in the federal government. Persons who received appointments in a previous administration may lose their positions in a new administration as a form of punishment for having supported the wrong candidate.

Supporters of the successful candidate to the nation's highest office, the presidency, seek their reward of employment by obtaining the endorsement of their local political leaders, party members, and others, preferably friends of the new president. They submit these recommendations, together with a formal application, to the White House for approval. Upon receipt, the applications are transferred to the agency in which the position is located. The favored applicants are then appointed to the desired positions.

The documents generated in this process constitute innumerable series of records (now on file in the National Archives), and they are identified as appointment papers, short-term applications, nominations, and recommendations. Such documents are grouped as a series of materials in the administrative records of nearly all federal agencies, excluding a few whose records were destroyed by fire or other causes.

Most series of appointment papers are arranged by presidential administration. Some are arranged by the position sought, the geographical area in which the position is located, and the office within the agency having the position. At least one series of records has applications filed under the name of the incumbent officeholder and the city or town in which the regional office is located. Sometimes documents relating to appointments are found in numerous routine correspondence series and in the records of other agencies.

Until the end of the nineteenth century, successful applicants received their official appointment papers or commissions through the Department of State, where the Great Seal of the United States was affixed to them. Federal agencies were later authorized to use their own agency seal on documents.

The volume of such records has not been computed because many collateral records series must be counted, eliminated, or selectively included in order to obtain a footage count. The collateral records series serve to document appointments and services when the actual appointment papers themselves are unavailable, incomplete, or inaccurate. Some collateral series are copies of attested confirmations or rejections made by the Senate. Others include oaths, commissions, resignations, declinations, withdrawals, registers, and order files that identify postmaster appointments.

Though there are many series of appointment papers and substitute records of nonmilitary federal agencies, the identification of blacks who received federal appointments cannot be made simply by examining the records and looking for telltale evidence such as descriptive terms, color designations, typical names, or other descriptives generally employed to ferret out blacks in public records.

The *Official Register of the United States,* commonly known as the Blue Book, was first published in 1816, and has been published biannually since 1817. Other registers such as the *Official Army Register,* the *Navy Register,* and the *Government Organization Manual* are helpful in identifying positions held by black federal employees and military officers. None of the registers, however, refers to race, color, or creed of the employee.

In spite of the handicaps and obstacles that exist in identifying black federal appointees, the reward can be great. The correspondence of individuals—and that of their supporters—who seek appointments may describe why they believe they merit the positions in order to counter the allegations from persons opposing their appointments. This is especially true of the letters of individuals who did not receive an appointment on their first application and of those who the administration particularly desired to be appointed. A single example of a file of appointment papers from the General Records of the Treasury Department (Record Group 56), will serve to illustrate the kind of information that is found in these records.

W.H. Williams of Lafayette, Louisiana, formerly an assistant weigher at the U.S. Customs House in New Orleans during the Arthur administration, sought an appointment as an assistant appraiser to the same customs house during the Benjamin Harrison administration. The file includes several letters from individuals, nearly all of which read as follows:

Sir:

We the undersigned members of the Third Congressional District Committee of the Parish of Lafourche, do respectfully ask the appointment of W.H. Williams at the Port of New Orleans, Louisiana. Mr. Williams has served the General government for three years and two months in the capacity of Assistant U.S. Weigher which position he filled with integrity and ability. His appointment would give satisfaction to this parish and district and also the State of Louisiana.

Respectfully,

/S/ J.T. Whitehurst[1]

A second letter contains three signatures, and a third, three pages of signatures, from not only local, but county and state party leaders. The fourth is a former application submitted by Williams two weeks after the letter of recommendation. He simply states:

Sir:

The undersigned respectfully submits his name as an applicant for the position of Assistant Appraiser at the Port of New Orleans, Louisiana, feeling assured that with the number of signers from all parts of the state, appended to my petition praying for the appointment, it would be satisfactory to the citizens of Lafayette, and to the State of Louisiana.

I am,
Very Respectfully,

W.H. Williams[2]

A third letter from Williams reads as follows:

Sir:

I visited your city about ten days ago with the expectation of having a short interview with you in regard to my application for Assistant Appraiser at the Port of New Orleans, Louisiana, but as you were away, I failed in my purpose.

He then renews his plea for an appointment and extols his demonstrated loyalty and virtues through reference to his former federal service, adding that:

On last April I passed the Civil Service Examination for Assistant Weigher reaching 93 percent, and the first on the list. This is sufficient test of my ability.

Now speaking politically, I think I can say without contradiction, that at the recent election held in the Third Congressional District on the 3rd inst., that there was not a parish in that district that did near as well as the Parish of Lafayette, not withstanding, as you are aware, of the troubles and the bulldozing that have been carried on there since a year. T. Paddis, Pres. Par. Committee and myself, secretary, are the ones by whose instrumentality the democratic majority was seduced and the largest republican vote polled at a Congressional election in that parish. Now to use the words of Gen. Badger who was a spectator at the Lafayette poll on election day: 'You and a few [other] colored men deserve much credit in this election. There is no telling the amount of persuasion it took to make those people vote.' This work was partly the reason why Gen. Badger, Judge Marks, Hon. A.H. Leonard, Col. Lewis, F.F. Suthon, and others whose names appear upon my petition praying for you to appoint me to the position spoken of.

Your most obedient and humble servant,

W.H. Williams[3]

Another letter from Williams outlines the many services he performed as a delegate to national conventions and local parish Republican committees:

> Sir:
> The work which was accomplished by myself and T. Paddis in Lafayette at the recent election for Congressman should never be forgotten by those who set a high estimate upon bravery, nerve and courage, which we exhibited, I think, in a considerable degree. Lafayette with her five hundred regulators and bulldozers, perambulating the streets every night before election, and in other sections, whipping, driving away, and even murdering did not deter us from securing the largest republican vote ever cast at an election for Congressman.

He ended his letter by saying:

> I am living away from home temporarily, on account of about two hundred regulators have come to and passed all through my house one night in search of a man, and I had three of them arrested, and the Mayor of the town fined them the full limit of the law. I expect to go back, as soon as I get some work, that is for my family.
>
> I am,
> Very Respectfully,
>
> W.H. Williams[4]

Not all appointment papers will reveal information on the times or conditions of an individual's appointment. Some of the papers, however, do provide information on many traits that are displayed by those opposed to the appointment of a given candidate.

Researchers are amazed at the value of appointment papers. Sometimes their search can unearth the totally unexpected. Such is a list of employees of the U.S. Customs House at New Orleans prepared by the Grand Army of the Republic and the Union League in 1880, which identified each employee by name, political affiliation, citizenship, and military service. Other lists include the appointing power, the sponsor for retention on the job, and general remarks.

Appointment papers can be a great source of black history. They have been used in the preparation of scholarly works, but their potential remains generally untapped.

NOTES

1. J.T. Whitehurst to President Benjamin Harrison, September 1, 1889, Appointment Papers File, Letters Received, Records of the Department of the Treasury, Record Group 56, National Archives Building, Washington, D.C.
2. W.H. Williams to President Benjamin Harrison, September 9, 1889, ibid.
3. W.H. Williams to President Benjamin Harrison, September 30, 1889, ibid.
4. W.H. Williams to President Benjamin Harrison, October 18, 1889, ibid.

Military Records for Nonmilitary History

PRESTON E. AMOS

Making use of military records for nonmilitary history may appear, on the surface, to be an impossibility, but this is not necessarily the case. Over a considerable number of years, I have spent hundreds of hours doing research on the fifty-seven known blacks that qualified for the Medal of Honor between 1863 and 1898.[1]

I began this task after seeing a television drama that was devoted to the Battle of the Crater, which was fought near Petersburg, Virginia. To lead this particular battle, Gen. Ambrose Burnside selected the black troops in his command and provided special training for them to carry out the assignment. One day before the battle, however, Gen. Ulysses S. Grant and George Meade ordered Burnside not to use the black troops to lead the assault. If it failed, Grant and Meade feared, they might be accused of trying to get rid of blacks by using them as "cannon fodder." Then, too, it could well have been that the good Generals Grant and Meade had grave doubts about the fighting abilities of the inexperienced and untried blacks in the Army of the Potomac. At any rate, Burnside was forced to substitute unprepared, battle-fatigued white troops at the last minute. The result was a fiasco. The Union forces lost the engagement and suffered 3,798 casualties, including 1,327 blacks, who had been ordered into the battle at a later stage.

That television program about the Battle of the Crater stirred me, and I decided to do research on the black recipients of the Medal of Honor. I read such books as Benjamin Quarles's *The Negro in the Civil War* and, in time, became a specialist in black Civil War history. From the Quarles book and others, I discovered that a number of black soldiers and sailors had won the Medal of Honor.

When I began my research I focused on the sixteen army men who qualified for the Medal of Honor during the Civil War. The National Archives records that I relied on most during this phase of the research were

1. the compiled service records of volunteer Union soldiers who served with the United States Colored Troops (Record Group 94);

2. correspondence and other records of the Adjutant General's Office (Record Group 94); and,

3. the pension files (Record Group 15).

The compiled service record of a soldier who served with the United States Colored Troops is enclosed in a jacket envelope and includes abstracts of his physical description, age, occupation at the time of enlistment, term of enlisted service, date and place of enlistment, date of promotion, medical record, date of discharge, and other information. The jacket envelope also includes the originals of papers relating solely to a particular soldier, such as volunteer enlistment records; substitute volunteer enlistment records; death reports; evidence of title of slave owners who filed for compensation for an enlisted slave; and certificates of disability for medical discharge of soldiers who became disabled. There is an alphabetical card index to these compiled service records on microfilm (M-589). Each index card lists the name of the soldier, his rank at the time of both his enlistment and his discharge, and the unit in which he served.

Also retained in the records of the Adjutant General's Office are the letters it received and sent, as well as the general correspondence of another War Department division: the short-lived Record and Pension Office.

The "Letters Received by the Adjutant General's Office" series covers such matters as the appointment, recruitment, transfers, pay, promotion, leave, discharge, and other personnel actions involving army officers and enlisted men. Orders, regulations, and other issuances of the War Department; military expeditions and campaigns; military installations and organizations; and Indian affairs are also found in this series. These letters, with enclosures, were received from army personnel, federal and state officials, members of Congress, private persons, and business firms. The letters are useful, and are located in a series of records that extends from 1800 to 1889. They are on microfilm (M-565, M-619, M-666, and M-689). The "Letters Sent by the Adjutant General's Office" series includes the very same types of correspondence as the "Letters Received" series. They cover the years 1800 to 1890 and are also on microfilm (M-565).

The "General Correspondence of the Record and Pension Office" series covers almost every subject relating to the service of volunteer organizations and to the officers and enlisted men who served in them. The correspondence includes requests for certificates of discharge; certificates in lieu of lost discharge papers; Medals of Honor for meritorious and distinguished services rendered; removal of charges of desertion; and information needed for admissions to homes for disabled soldiers. This office was able to supply such information. On microfilm there is an *Index to General Correspondence of the Record and Pension Office* that covers the years 1889 to 1904 (T-288).

The Adjutant General's Office and the Record and Pension Office are separate record groups. Only from 1889 to 1904 was there a difference. During this fifteen-year period, the Adjutant General's Office was responsible for records of the regular army and matters relating to such documents. On the other hand, the Record and Pension Office had custody of records of volunteer forces and all business relating to them. The Record and Pension Office and the Adjutant General's Office were later consolidated.

The records of the Adjutant General's Office and the Record Pension Office provide very valuable information about black army men who qualified for the Medal of Honor during the Civil War. The most useful information, however, is found in the pension files. As one National Archives publication states, "A pension file contains some or all of the following: the name, military or naval record; his age or the date of his birth; date and place of marriage; date and place of his death; the maiden name of his wife; the date of her death, and the names of those surviving children with the date and place of birth of each."[2]

The value of the pension files cannot be overestimated. These files contain a gold mine of useful information and without them it would not have been possible to reconstruct the lives of my subjects to the extent that I have. Fortunately, many veterans or their heirs filed for pensions at one time or another after the Civil War. Veterans with service-connected disabilities were eligible for pensions, and their wives and their children under sixteen became eligible after the veterans' deaths. If a serviceman died while still on active duty, his dependents qualified for a pension.

Every veteran or dependent who filed for a pension did not receive one. Often it could not be proved that an injury or disability was service

OVERLEAF:

A widow's pension application, June 6, 1908. (RG 94, Adjutant General's Office)

DECLARATION OF A WIDOW FOR ORIGINAL PENSION.

STATE OF *Tennessee*

County of *Fayette* } *ss.:*

On this *6th* day of *June*, A. D. one thousand eight hundred and ninety- *1908* personally appeared before me, a *Justice of the Peace*, within and for the county and State aforesaid, *Delilah Turner*, aged *86* years, a resident of the _____ of *LaGrange* county of *Fayette* State of *Tennessee*, who being duly sworn according to law, makes the following declaration in order to obtain a pension under the acts of Congress granting pension to the widows of soldiers and sailors who have died by reason of wound or injury received, or disease contracted, in the service of the United States and in the line of duty:

That she is the widow of *Frank Jones*, who was

_____ under the name of " "
[Enrolled or commissioned.]

at _____ on the _____ day of _____, 18____

as a _____ in *Co H 59 U.S.C. Inf.*
[Here state rank and designation of organization or name of vessel.]

and was discharged on the _____ day of _____, 18____.

and who died *in Guntown battle* on the _____ day of _____,

18____, of _____ due to *wounds*
[Here state the immediate cause of death.]

incurred in the above named service.

That she was married under the name of *Delilah Jackson* to said soldier

at *Jones Farm* on the _____ day of _____, 18____,

by *the custom in time of slavery*; that there was no legal barrier to the marriage;

that she had *not* been previously married; that the soldier had *not* been previously married.

[If there was a prior marriage of either, the date and place of death or divorce of former consort or consorts should be stated.]

That she has _____ remarried since the death of the said soldier, *to Robert*
[If remarried, the date and place of remarriage should be stated.]

Turner on 1868

That the said soldier left the following named children under 16 years of age at the date of his death, to-wit:

Turner Armstrong E Jones born *21st Jany.* 18*60*, at *Jones Farm*

_____ born _____, 18____, at _____

_____ born _____, 18____, at _____

_____ born _____, 18____, at _____

_____ born _____, 18____, at _____

_____ born _____, 18____, at _____

[If any child has died since the soldier's death, its name and the date of its death should be stated. If soldier left no children, the claimant should so state.]

That she has _____ heretofore applied for pension.
[If prior application has been made, the number thereof, the service on

which it was based, and the name of the soldier should be stated.]

That she hereby appoints with full power of substitution and revocation,

WM. FLETCHER & CO., of Washington, D. C.,

her true and lawful attorneys to prosecute this claim.

That her POST OFFICE ADDRESS is No. _____ Street.

City of *LaGrange* County of *Fayette*, State of *Tennessee*

Claimant's signature *Delilah X Turner*
mark

Attest: 1. _____

2. *J. W. Hunt*

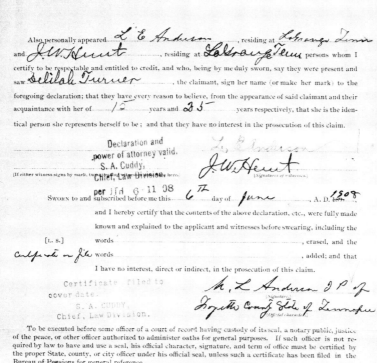

Also personally appeared *L. E. Anderson*, residing at *Lagrange, Tenn* and *J. W. Hunt*, residing at *Lagrange, Tenn* persons whom I certify to be respectable and entitled to credit, and who, being by me duly sworn, say they were present and saw *Delilah Turner*, the claimant, sign her name (or make her mark) to the foregoing declaration; that they have every reason to believe, from the appearance of said claimant and their acquaintance with her of *15* years and *25* years respectively, that she is the identical person she represents herself to be ; and that they have no interest in the prosecution of this claim.

Declaration and power of attorney valid.
S. A. Cuddy,
Chief, Law Division.
[If either witness signs by mark, two persons who write sign only here.]

L. E. Anderson
J. W. Hunt +
[Signatures of witnesses.]

per jfd 6-11 08

SWORN to and subscribed before me this *6th* day of *June*, A. D. *1908*, and I hereby certify that the contents of the above declaration, etc., were fully made known and explained to the applicant and witnesses before swearing, including the

[L. S.]   words _____, erased, and the
Certificate on file words _____, added; and that
I have no interest, direct or indirect, in the prosecution of this claim.

Certificate filed to cover date.
S. A. CUDDY,
Chief, Law Division.

M. L. Anderson J P of
Fayette County State of Tennessee
[Official character.]

To be executed before some officer of a court of record having custody of its seal, a notary public, justice of the peace, or other officer authorized to administer oaths for general purposes. If such officer is not required by law to have and use a seal, his official character, signature, and term of office must be certified by the proper State, county, or city officer under his official seal, unless such a certificate has been filed in the Bureau of Pensions for general reference.

Testimony in support of allegations made in a declaration may be taken before any officer whose authority and signature are duly certified, and who shall disclaim any interest, direct or indirect, in the prosecution of the claim.

WIDOW'S CLAIM FOR PENSION.
ORIGINAL.

Claimant, *Delilah Turner.*
Soldier, *Grant Jones.*
Co. *K* Reg't *9* Vol. 18
Enlisted, ____
Discharged, ____

WM. FLETCHER & CO.,
Pension and Claims Attorneys,
WASHINGTON, D. C.

connected. But, even so, the pension application and the evidence submitted with it can be extremely useful to a biographer.

In examining the pension files of my subjects, I was constantly amazed at the different kinds of valuable information available in them. Birth certificates, marriage certificates, death certificates, affidavits of all types and, in some instances, even newspaper clippings about and a few photographs of my subjects were found. The pension files are indexed on microfilm (M-686).

In addition to the army men that qualified for the Medal of Honor, eight navy men also qualified. Although the navy's records are not as extensive as the army's, a great deal of valuable information about navy men can be obtained. The naval records that I relied on most during my research were the muster rolls and the pension files, which contain the following information about each sailor: name, rating, date and length of enlistment, place, or ship received from, place of birth, age, occupation before enlistment, complexion, color of eyes and hair, height, and remarks such as when and where he may have been transferred or discharged.

The same type of information found in the muster rolls and pension files is also available in the "Enlistment Rendezvous" records. Locating the information in this source, however, is a difficult task. The date of a sailor's enlistment must be known before it can be determined where the sailor is listed in the "Enlistment Rendezvous" records.

The pension files for navy men are just as valuable to the researcher as those for army men. Both contain the same type of useful information. Fortunately, some of the black navy men who earned the Medal of Honor during the War of the Rebellion filed for pensions, and, of course, the material gleaned from their pensions files is being utilized by researchers.

During the period of the Indian wars, a total of eighteen black army men qualified for the Medal of Honor. Fourteen of these soldiers belonged to three of the four black Regular Army regiments that Congress authorized after the Civil War. The other four soldiers belonged to an army detachment known as the Seminole-Negro Indian Scouts. (The story of the relationship between the Seminoles and blacks is one of the most fascinating chapters in black history. Fugitive slaves joined the Seminole Indians in Florida and ended up in the American Southwest and Mexico with the same Indians.)

Sixteen of the eighteen blacks earned the medal for fighting Indians in Texas, Arizona, New Mexico, and Colorado. The other two received the Medal of Honor for gallantry in fighting the white bandits who robbed an army paymaster that the soldiers were escorting in Arizona.

The fight with the bandits illustrates how archival records can be used to correct distortions in black history. The following is the version recorded by an Arizona settler in his memoirs, which were published in 1915:

> On May 11th, 1889, the Army Paymaster, Major Wham, started to drive from Fort Grant to San Carlos, with about $65,000 in a safe. He had a guard of Negro troops, riding in advance. . . . The major set [sic] on the front seat with the driver and never felt more secure in his life.
>
> When they had driven to the west end of the Graham Mountains, on Cedar Springs Road, a volley of shots rang out. The leading mule was shot down, stopping the wagon. The negro guards, both in front and rear decided it would be best to move on, which they did—like a flock of blackbirds leaving a corn field.[3]

When I read this account at the Library of Congress, I knew the author had distorted the incident, since I was aware that two of the soldiers had received the Medal of Honor for bravery in the battle and had not run away at the sound of the first shot. That was almost all I knew about the affair, however. At the National Archives, I found the report of the incident that Maj. Joseph W. Wham, the paymaster, had submitted to the secretary of war on September 1, 1889. In the report, Major Wham stated that two of the black soldiers did little or no fighting and almost immediately left the field. The other ten men remained and fought in the gun battle, which lasted about thirty minutes. Eight of the ten were wounded—two of them twice—and the major reported that "all behaved in the most courageous and heroic manner." The major stated that he had served in the Civil War regiment that Ulysses S. Grant had once commanded as a colonel, and the regiment was justly proud of its record of sixteen battles. "But," he concluded, "I never witnessed better courage or better fighting than shown by those colored soldiers, on May 11th 1889, as the bullet marks on the robbers' positions today abundantly attest."[4]

The National Archives has several types of records on both regular army soldiers and Indian scouts that contain useful information for the biographer. Among these records are the enlistment papers (Record Group 94), correspondence and other records of the Adjutant General's Office, the old reliable pension files, and a few miscellaneous records that deserve a passing mention.

An enlistment paper normally shows the name of the enlisted man; his place of birth; age, occupation; the date and place of his enlistment or reenlistment; the period for which he enlisted; and his personal description. The enlistment papers of most soldiers are in separate jackets that also include his hospital and death and burial records, if death occurred in the service.

The registers of enlistments are large volumes that summarize the information in the enlistment papers. The registers of enlistments usually cover all army enlistments for a period of a year or more. Entries are arranged alphabetically by the initial letter of the given name. Each entry in a register relates to a single enlistment and is recorded on one line extending across two facing pages. A full entry shows the name of the enlisted man; the date, place, and period of his enlistment or reenlistment; the name of the town, country, or state where he was born; his occupation and personal description; the designation of his regiment and company; his performance evaluation; and the date and nature of his separation from the service. The registers of enlistment are on microfilm (M-233).

The following record groups are somewhat useful in researching soldiers who fought in campaigns against Indians in the West: the monthly returns from the Regular Army cavalry regiments, 1733-1916 (Record Group 94, M-744); the monthly returns from Regular Army infantry regiments, June 1821-December 1916 (Record Group 94, M-665); and the monthly returns from U.S. military posts, 1800-1916 (Record Group 94, M-617).

Both the monthly returns from cavalry and infantry regiments contain the names of absent enlisted men and the reasons for their absence; the names of enlisted men lost or gained and the reasons; the names of enlisted men on extra or daily duty and the nature of the duty; records of events; total strength of the regiments by rank; stations of the regiments and their companies; and other information. These returns, as previously indicated above, are on microfilm.

The returns from U.S. military posts include morning reports, field returns, rosters of officers, and related papers, which were added to the collection by the Adjutant General's Office either as supplementary information or as substitutes for missing post returns. Field returns, for example, generally show the movement of troops or detachments to and from the post or station or give information concerning detachments in the field from units stationed at the post. Among the related papers are cards that contain information pertaining to wars and skirmishes with the Indians.

While a number of blacks were becoming heroes in the army out West, a number were also becoming heroes in the navy. During what is referred to as the "interim" from 1871 to the beginning of the Spanish-American War in 1898, seven black seamen qualified for the Medal of Honor—including five that I discovered by systematically checking the navy Medal of Honor list against the muster rolls. Those five individuals had never been identified as blacks.[5] At one time the navy presented the medal to men who saved drowning persons, and all seven of the sailors received medals because of such life-saving. The muster rolls and the pension files are the main sources that I used in gathering information about the seven black navy heroes of the interim period. During the Spanish-American War of 1898, six blacks qualified for the Medal of Honor—five soldiers and one sailor. The various records already described provide more than enough information about those gallant men.

No blacks received the medal during the two world wars. Two soldiers qualified for it during the Korean conflict, and fifteen soldiers and five marines during the Vietnam conflict. However, the National Archives was not able to make information available about these men because of the restriction on the use of military records less than seventy-five years old. This restriction did not impede the research because I was able to obtain all the information that was needed, including photographs, from the military services themselves.

NOTES

1. Shortly after this paper was presented, another black recipient of the Medal of Honor was uncovered through the use of National Archives records. He was Seaman Alphonse Girandy, who qualified for it aboard the U.S.S. *Petrel* on 31 March, 1901. The uncovering of Seaman Girandy necessitates the revision of numerous publications which state that the two black recipients of the medal during the Korean Conflict were the first to receive it since the Spanish-American War. (Sgt. Maj. Edward Lee Baker received a Medal of Honor on 3 July, 1902, but the action qualifying him for the award occurred on 1 July, 1898.)
2. Meredith B. Colket and Frank Bridgers, comp., *Guide to Genealogical Records in the National Archives* (Washington, D.C.: Government Printing Office, 1964), p. 85.
3. Edward Wilson, *An Unwritten History* (Phoenix, Ariz.: The McNeil Co., 1915), p. 39.
4. Maj. Joseph W. Wham to the Secretary of War, September 1, 1889, Letters Received by the Office of the Adjutant General (Main Series), 1881-1889, National Archives Microfilm Publication, M-689, frames 112-114.
5. Shortly after presenting this paper at the conference, it was learned that Geraldine N. Phillips of the National Archives had also discovered the same five recipients at approximately the same time I discovered them. As a result, I cannot take full credit for uncovering them. The credit must be shared with Ms. Phillips. The fruits of her long and hard labor are found in *Documents Relating to the Military and Naval Service of Blacks Awarded the Congressional Medal of Honor from the Civil War to the Spanish-American War,* a National Archives microfilm publication pamphlet describing the contents of M-929.

Freedmen's Bureau Records: Texas, a Case Study

BARRY A. CROUCH

Three years after the National Archives officially opened in 1935, a short article appeared in the *Journal of Negro History* that discussed some of the Archives' holdings in relation to the Negro. The Bureau of Refugees, Freedmen, and Abandoned Lands, commonly known as the Freedmen's Bureau, was not even mentioned. A decade later, Roland C. McConnell, pursuing the same topic in an article, noted that the records of the bureau contained such "material for both headquarters and field offices as reports on Freedmen's camps; labor contracts; distribution of rations, clothing, and medicine; abandoned lands; aid to schools; arrests and outrages; and the care of refugees."[1] The McConnell article provided simply a listing and nothing more.

More recently, however, David Donald, a well-known Reconstruction scholar, has asserted that historians know "all too little about what Negroes wanted" during this turbulent period. Since there are few written sources by blacks for this era, we must turn to manuscripts that, while not wholly adequate, are the major contemporary viewpoints for the first years of freedom for the former bondspeople. These records, Donald contends, "are exceedingly revealing. The voluminous Freedmen's Bureau papers in the National Archives are one of the most important sources in Negro history—not the papers of the head of the bureau and his chief agents, but those of the agents in the field, in Huntsville, Alabama, and Lynchburg, Virginia."[2]

Donald, as many historians now realize, is essentially correct. To comprehend black aspirations during Reconstruction, the indispensable place to begin one's research is the Freedmen's Bureau records. This, of course, does not mean they should not be supplemented with other records, such as the manuscript census returns, army manuscripts, plantation records, personal papers, and local government records. But the indication is that for far too long the bureau material has been used, in many cases, for all the wrong reasons.[3] Bureau sources, like other manuscripts, can be misunderstood and misused if the wrong questions are asked. Possibly, a brief examination of bureau records can establish some of the most important contributions they provide for viewing the black community.

Before suggesting what treasures the bureau materials hold, it should be noted that they, like so many other early records about blacks, are essentially, though not exclusively, white sources. The skillful historian can, however, use the observations of whites to reveal much about black behavior which the observers themselves did not understand, but nevertheless reported. For example, our basic view of slavery has been taken from the plantation manuscripts left by the planters. Only now are we fully realizing and using the slave narratives and fugitive slave accounts to their full effectiveness; John W. Blassingame's book and Eugene D. Genovese's work are but the foremost examples.[4]

The bureau records do have one inestimable advantage that plantation sources do not: they contain numerous letters and accounts written by and to blacks. And since blacks were involved in the bureau as agents, inspectors, and teachers, their ideas and outlooks serve to balance what was predominantly a white agency. Moreover, pressure exerted by the black community on bureau personnel sometimes forced agents to shift their perspective toward that of the freedmen.

A perusal of bureau records might start where the blacks themselves began, with freedom. It is important to understand how and when emancipation came for the slaves, but of equal importance is the conception blacks held of genuine freedom. Freedmen brought with them from slavery aspirations which included a desire for land, education, and independence. The culture which had sustained blacks throughout slavery was to be creatively employed in the new circumstances of freedom; clearly they were not a people rendered passive and dependent by slavery.[5]

Emancipation did not automatically begin for all slaves on the magic date, January 1, 1863. Freedom began in 1861 for slaves at Port Royal, South Carolina, but it was not until June 19, 1865, that slaves were officially freed in Texas. In Kentucky, slavery was not legally abolished until the ratification of the Thirteenth Amendment in December 1865. Throughout the war freedom came to many slaves as the Union Army advanced into their homeland, or as the slaves left the plantations and sought safety behind army lines. Freedom was a gradual and halting process and blacks themselves were instrumental in destroying the hated institution.

For example, in Kentucky, which remained a loyal slave state despite the Emancipation Proclamation, slavery as an institution was severely undermined by the slaves themselves long before freedom was legally attained. Some "masters" were forced to pay wages to their "slaves" to keep them at work. As one army man explained the situation, the black worker simply refused to labor and "allow his would-be master [to] receive the proceeds." One Kentuckian complained that the old slavery laws had ceased to have any control over the blacks, and owners could no longer discipline them "except in but few instances where slaves remain at home . . . by being paid a fair compensation by their owners."[6]

A prevailing concept, so long a standard of Reconstruction history, was the idea that blacks left the plantations when they were freed and congregated as a destitute and hopeless drain on the cities. The bureau records contain numerous complaints by whites on this theme.[7] Few ever questioned why the freedmen were traveling over the South, and, at times, gathering in the cities. There are several explanations for this mass movement.

As any overworked bureau agent could have pointed out, blacks were trying to reunite their families and find relatives. The exigencies of slavery often divided slave families, and the natural response when freedom finally came was to search for long-missing relatives. There must have been unbounded joy in many of their hearts when an agent notified them of the location of a family member who had not been seen for years. Blacks, of course, also sought out family relations on their own.[8]

Other factors were also involved in the physical movement of the black population. Many slaves had been sent to other states for safekeeping during the war. Texas serves as a prime example. The state was not successfully invaded and slavery remained relatively intact until Gen. E. Kirby Smith surrendered in May 1865. Naturally many blacks desired to return to a familiar home and family after the forced movement during the war, or else they were simply looking for a better economic situation.[9]

The former masters also forced movement among the blacks. In Saint Charles parish Louisiana James W. McCutcheon simply ran off all the slaves and abandoned his property when the Union naval fleet arrived. Similar episodes were common all over the South. Thomas W. Conway, the assistant commissioner of the bureau, remarked that McCutcheon and his type were among the "most malignant rebels of this region, and should not be forgiven too readily." Despite Conway's protestations, McCutcheon's land was later restored to him. In Texas, there were reports that many planters in Robertson and Burleson counties were selling their crops and leaving the state without paying their black workers.[10]

Finally, another compelling reason that blacks moved was simply to test their new freedom. After the restraints upon free movement dictated by slavery, the basic right to travel at will, to leave one's master, was the act of a free man. The same can be said for the indisputable tendency to gather in cities: blacks believed they had a larger area of freedom, self-determination, and the general support and security of a black community.[11]

As the former bondspeople moved into their new roles, the problems they encountered were many and varied. The difficulties blacks faced as free people included the significant one of evolving an independent way of life within the context of continued economic domination by whites. Most blacks would have desired to avoid this context by having their own land. Blacks were not generally able to have their own land in the South, and in places like Texas, where there was very little abandoned land, blacks were able to purchase only small parcels. In agricultural areas, as opposed to the cities, the contract labor, and later sharecropping, systems were instituted. A systematic analysis of the agricultural situation in the South during Reconstruction is badly needed.

Although the Freedmen's Bureau played a major role in encouraging blacks to sign contracts, many agents—contrary to some accounts—did realize the pitfalls of this particular method. One agent in Houston noted that blacks seemed to fear that in signing their names to contracts they were bartering away their freedom—a realistic assessment of their position in relation to their employers.[12]

Evidence indicates that the freedmen resisted not work, but work in a form which undermined their independence and freedom. A superintendent of freedmen in Louisiana observed astutely that blacks' objections to the contract system "consisted chiefly" of the fact that "they had *no confidence whatever* in the word of their 'old masters.' " They believed that they could not "trust the power that has never accorded [blacks] any privileges" and that their "former oppressors show by their actions that they would sooner retard than advance [blacks'] prosperity." In nine out of ten cases, the agent continued, blacks acceded to "fair terms for their labor" when it was explained by a government agent; "exactly in the same ratio did they refuse to listen to any proposition made by the planter alone. . . . The disposition to be idle, formed no part of the reason for their refusing to contract with their 'former masters.' "[13]

The widespread preference for buying, contracting, or sharecropping land—rather than more dependent wage labor—is only another indication of many attempts to be as free from white supervision as possible. Aversion to working for the old master reflected their concept of independence. The freedmen resisted even bureau regulations if they did not allow enough latitude for an independent status.

Even if distrust of the white employer were overcome, many complexities remained in the contractual relationship. Since what little medical care slaves had received was dependent upon the planter, what did blacks do during those first few years of freedom in this sphere? Migration to Texas involved numerous health hazards for the freedmen because it was a new area and there were ecological differences. On their home plantations during slavery, lack of mobility prevented, to some extent, exposure to outside health hazards. During the process of emancipation, however, large masses of people—armies, blacks, guerilla bands, returning soldiers—brought everyone into contact with unfamiliar diseases.[14]

On the plantation the slave had a stable, if monotonous, food supply. Migration to a different section, through force or escape, required blacks to forage for their food, unless, of course, they had taken provisions with them. Wartime destruction and unfamiliar terrain made scavenging difficult, and increased the possibility of exposure to disease-bearing animals. Inadequate and uncertain food supply, lack of shelter, stress and fatigue inherent in migration, and exposure to a host of unfamiliar germs all contributed greatly to physical breakdown, and ultimately to the inability of blacks to work and fulfill contracts.[15]

Texas seemed to have faced perennially a labor shortage, and constant efforts were made to bring more black laborers into the state, especially from South Carolina. During 1867 while these labor importations were taking place, Texas was seized with yellow fever and cholera epidemics, whose victims included the assistant commissioner of the bureau. In short, the migrations that occurred in the South during and after the war must be considered in the light of health factors, and although the bureau records do not contain vast quantities of materials on this subject, they do give important clues and leads as to how blacks, and whites, fared in an environment disrupted by war and at times ravaged by plagues.[16]

One last question remains in relation to the problems of health: what kind of medical care did blacks receive as freedpeople, and can it be compared to the care they had received from the planters during slavery? Before slavery was abolished, the planter considered his chattel an investment; after emancipation the planter's concern was limited to the length of a contract, and many times not even that. As a result, the demand for physicians decreased and perhaps blacks were forced to rely more on their own community resources rather than upon whites. To be sure, under the contract labor system, many planters did stipulate that they would be responsible for medical care, and the bureau attempted to hold them to this promise, but generally this system of medical care was probably a failure.[17]

The Freedmen's Bureau itself provided some medical help for blacks just after the war, establishing hospitals and infirmaries in several states. But most of those receiving aid were indigent and older black people who could not fend for themselves. These hospitals also became dumping grounds for the insane and unstable. The duration of care was short, and many were probably released little better off than when they had been admitted.

Health care is a major social force, and more intensive analysis of the health services the freedmen received, and the way they developed provisions for their own medical care needs to be investigated. The bureau records are spotty on this particular subject, but they do provide some indication in several states, notably Louisiana, of what was or was not being done to meet the health care needs of blacks during the early years of Reconstruction.[18]

Another aspect of the living conditions of the freedpeople that requires more thorough investigation is the type of housing they were able to obtain or occupy during the postwar years. Bureau agents were not in a position to do anything about the appalling "houses" blacks were compelled to live in, but they often commented upon them. Again, in contrast to their attitudes during slavery, the planters were not so concerned with where or how blacks lived, just so they worked the crops and a sizeable yield was returned. Many blacks were so mired in poverty that they probably lived little better, if any better, than during slavery days.[19]

One aspect of black life that the bureau records do divulge in detail is crimes committed by and against blacks. The extent of unlawful acts is hard to ascertain because whites used the laws to their own ends and were able to isolate effectively many blacks whom they found recalcitrant. Because of

OVERLEAF:

Pages from an 1867 inspection report of the Texas State Penitentiary describing the prisoners' sentences and the nature of their crimes. The report is from inspector of the prison, William H. Sinclair, to the Texas State authorities. (RG 105, Bureau of Refugees, Freedmen, and Abandoned Lands)

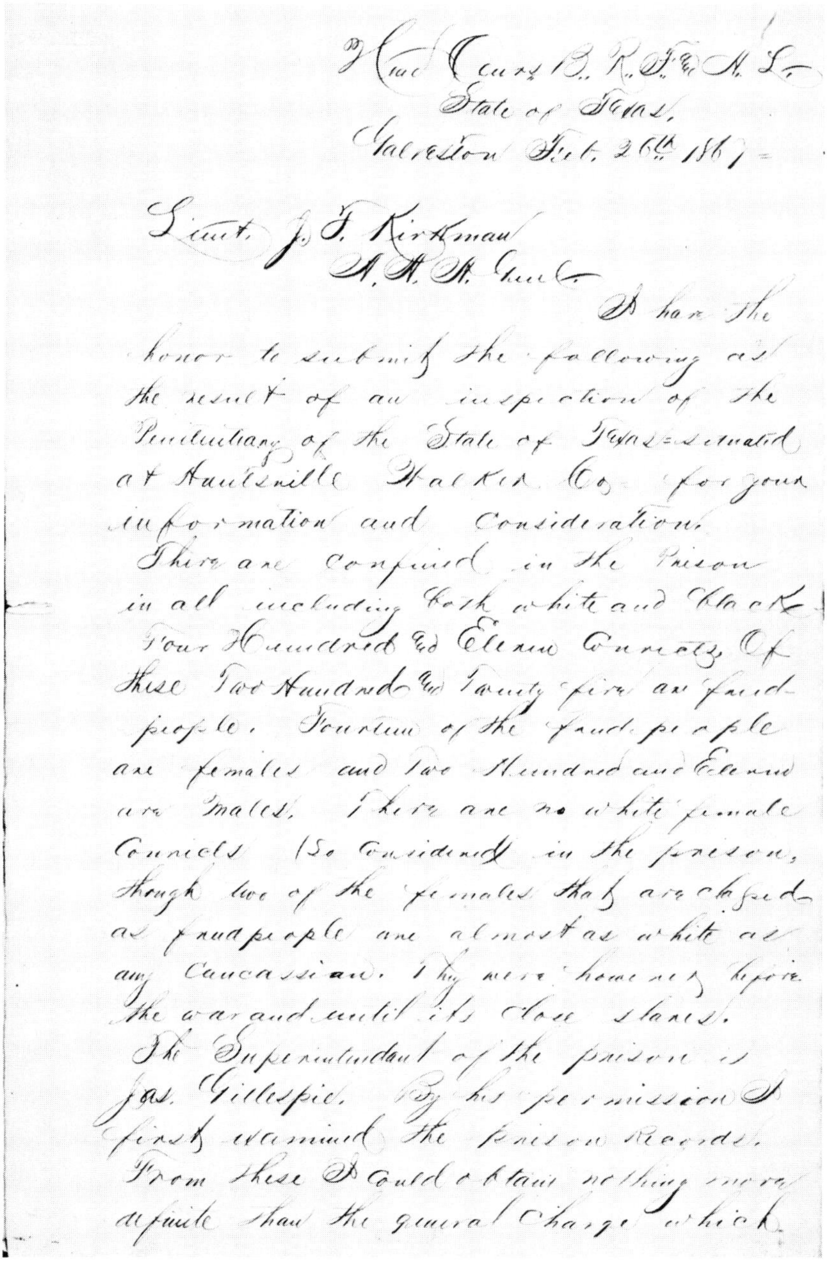

Head Quarters B. R. F. & A. L.
State of Texas,
Galveston Feb. 26th 1867.

Lieut. J. T. Kirkman
A. A. A. Genl.

I have the honor to submit the following as the result of an inspection of the Penitentiary of the State of Texas situated at Huntsville Walker Co. for your information and consideration.

There are confined in the Prison in all including both white and black Four Hundred and Eleven Convicts. Of these Two Hundred and Twenty five are freed-people. Fourteen of the freed-people are females and Two Hundred and Eleven are males. There are no white female Convicts (So Considered) in the prison, though two of the females that are classed as freedpeople are almost as white as any Caucassian. They were however before the war and until its close slaves.

The Superintendent of the prison is Jas. Gillespie. By his permission I first examined the Prison Records. From these I could obtain nothing more definite than the general charge which

Had they half the friends that many a greater
rascal has they would not remain in prison
one week, unfortunately they have not—
I see by the report of the Asst. Comr—
of Alabama (May. Genl. W. Swayne) a copy of which is herewith annexed that
the Penitentiary of that State became filled
with said people under almost the
same circumstances as was this one and
that the Gov. of the state upon having his
attention called to the fact and the circumstances
under which they were arrested and convicted
being properly presented to him issued
an almost universal pardon. I believe
that three fourths of the said people now
Confined at Huntsville are proper sub
-jects for the Executive Clemency of the
Gov. of this state. I cannot think that
he is aware of the actual condition of affairs
else he would pardon them. This investigation
has worked in their breasts hopes of pardon
and release. That the matter may not end with
this report is my earnest prayer for if
ever people deserved the assistance of
friends these do— Respectfully inviting your
attention to the annexed report

      I am Very Resp.
      Your Ob't. Servant
      Wm. H. Sinclair
      Inspector B. R. F. & A. L.

List of Freedwomen and Men Confined at Texas State Penitentiary at Huntsville Walker Co. giving name of County and particulars in each case as stated by them.

No	Name	County	Accusation	Sentence	Remarks
1	Jane Grisham	Brazos	Stealing $10.00	2 yrs	Has small child Babe
2	Carrie Petty	Smith	" Dresses	5 "	Has Babe – A cousin took her dresses and thus Carrie took a accusing
3	Rosa Moore	Upshur	Stealing Hog	2 "	Husband stole hog. Rose knew nothing of it – meat was found but her house and she made party – She + husband is in prison.
4	Georgia Swanson	Harrison	" Night Gown	2 "	Took it wash but did not return it – This girl is probably white but was a slave.
5	Elvira Mays	"	Helping prisoner to escape	2 "	Gave her husband a pick axe to get out of jail
6	Eliza Milsted	Goliad	Stealing 2 dresses and Earring	2 "	
7	Patty Ann Jennings	Harris	Stealing $80.00	3 "	Mistress owed her and would not pay her
8	Judy Hammond	Coryell	Burglary	2 "	White woman Jane Haynes persuaded her to break into store and accompanied her White woman not arrested
9	Fanny Fitzer	McLennan	Stealing $10.0	2 "	Found it upon table of lady for whom she was working
10	Caroline Williams	Cherokee	" wearing apparel $14.00	2 "	Taken from Mistress
11	Amanda Hawkins	Fayette	" $2.50	2 "	" " Washwoman
12	Caroline Johnson	Galveston	" An Petticoat	2 "	" " Mistress
13	Mary Chamlin	DeWitt	" shirt, pr of stocking and gas domestic	2 "	Admits it
14	Mary Burns	Gonzales	Stealing	2 "	Bed clothing 20 row as taken from employer she accused of it – denied it – She and her daughter both hung up by neck 2nd to me daughter acquitted, Convicted on daughter, claimed – Denies it

an investigation by a Texas bureau agent, it is possible to look fairly closely at prisoners incarcerated in the state penitentiary at Huntsville, Texas, in 1867. In total there were 411 convicts; 225 were freedpeople. There were no white women in the prison, but 14 black women were confined. The average sentence for all blacks was three years and sixty-four days. In what is a truly remarkable document, the bureau inspector interviewed each black person in the penitentiary, listing name, county of residence, alleged offense, and sentence.[20]

As can be imagined, some of the crimes were trivial and the attendant sentences unreasonably severe. Rose Moore of Upshur County, for instance, was serving two years for allegedly stealing a pig. Her husband had in fact stolen the hog and she knew nothing about it, but, unlike the movie *Sounder,* the meat was found in her house and so she was made a party to the crime. In another case, Jane Haynes, a white woman, had induced Judy Hammer of Coryell County to break into a store and even accompanied her. Haynes was not arrested but Hammer received two years for burglary. Elvira Mays was serving two years for giving her husband a pickaxe so he could escape jail, and Georgia Swanson received the same sentence for allegedly stealing a nightgown. Swanson had taken the gown home to wash it but had not returned it. The inspector's comment was that "this girl is probably white—but was a slave."[21]

Perhaps the most sensational case recorded in these documents, although not the longest sentence served by a black, was that of Isaiah Bragwell of Grimes County, who was serving ten years for stabbing a white man. The facts of the case were these: Bragwell stated that he "ran off" after his time of service was completed, though his employer wanted him to contract again. Bragwell left, but after only a half a mile his former employer caught up with him and tried to take him back. The white man then stopped and said "now G__d D__mn you you won't [*sic*] work for me and you shant work for anybody else," and drew a pistol. Bragwell then consented to work for him another year and for nothing if he would not kill him. The white man said, "no G__d d__n you you ran away and I am not going to let you live with anybody," and shot him through the left shoulder. Bragwell then stabbed the man, cutting him severely, and after stabbing him the "first time he kept on doing it he was so desperate."[22]

It is interesting to note that the three longest terms were for rather disparate crimes. Daniel Swarnuigen of Orange County and Joe Smith of McLennan County were both serving twenty years, the former for killing another black man in a drunken row, and the latter for murdering a black woman, although he denied it. Smith did have, the agent commented, a "bad temper." Jacob Falk was sentenced to fifteen years for attempted rape. Falk apparently wanted to steal his employer's gun and was caught in a room in which four persons were sleeping. David Bradley, who said he was arrested only on suspicion, was serving twelve years for burglary.[23]

Interviewer William H. Sinclair asserted that the general charge against blacks was theft and that the "whole cause of the prosecution has for its foundation malice, and is followed up on a spirit of revenge by men embittered, disappointed and foiled by the failure of their schemes. These convicts are the innocent and unfortunate victims of their wrath and disappointment." Sinclair stated he did not believe that all the statements submitted to him were correct and truthful but he was "fully convinced" that "any person listening to their simple, frank statements and looking into the black and honest faces could not believe otherwise."[24]

During slavery, such crimes would have been punished by the lash. "The trivial nature of the crimes charged against them," he continued, "and the severity of the punishment already inflicted upon them (even had they in every instance willfully and maliciously committed the crime) should be and are of themselves a sufficient argument for their release and are most assuredly a strong appeal for our assistance in relieving them if such a thing be possible."[25] Whether Sinclair was able to persuade the governor to grant executive clemency is not known, but surely his concern was sincere.

On the local level, bureau agents kept statistics concerning crimes committed by whites against blacks and by blacks against blacks. To deny that the black community had its own share of crime is, of course, pure nonsense. Many examples could be given but usually the cases involved drunkeness, disturbing the peace, or general rowdiness. A typical month's case load in Houston included forty-nine cases of debt, one of theft, three of assault and battery, and one of assault. Most complaints by blacks to the bureau concerned nonpayment of money for services rendered, difficulties in receiving the stipulated share of the crop, or violence committed by a white against a black. Agents also monitored the civil courts in an often futile effort to secure fair trials for blacks. In some instances, the agent, when allowed, removed the case from the hands of civil authorities.[26]

Sometimes bureau cases had humorous aspects. In Austin, James Haynes, a white man, complained to the bureau agent that Fletcher Burnet, a ten-year-old white boy, had had "carnal connection with one of his ewes." The only witness to this bizarre occurrence had been Lee Reed, a thirteen-year-old black lad. Haynes reported the incident to the agent because state law would not allow Reed to testify and Haynes therefore believed his only recourse was the bureau.[27] There was no indication of what happened to the boy or the ewe. Cases of this nature, however, were few and far between. Most were of a serious consequence and were so treated by bureau personnel.

One of the more interesting research possibilities of the bureau records, and one which Herbert Gutman has explored effectively in his book, *The Black Family in Slavery and Freedom, 1750-1925,* is examination of the status and stability of black families during Reconstruction. A chief function of the bureau, though little noted, was the reunification of black families after the war, with the bureau serving as a clearinghouse for all the southern states. When an agent received an inquiry about a certain black who was supposedly in his vicinity, he relayed the word to the black community and announcements were made during church services and other social gatherings. In certain respects, this was merely an extension of the slave grapevine that was so effective in transmitting information during the antebellum years. Many times it was successful, and the bureau would pay transportation expenses for the black to be reunited with his or her family.[28]

Just after the war, many black children in Texas and elsewhere had been separated from their parents. The practice of apprenticing or binding out the children to whites became rather common in Texas, and probably other states, before the bureau became fully established. In Texas, at least, the bureau let this practice continue temporarily, but then allowed it only in unusual circumstances. When the children were apprenticed, an advertisement was printed in the newspaper indicating what was being done and stating that if there were any objections, parents or relatives could contest the action. Tragically, many of the blacks could not read and so were unaware of what was taking place. In many instances, however, the children were returned to relatives or parents, and the Texas bureau records are filled with letters ordering whites to return children. Whites obviously saw in the apprenticeship system an opportunity to obtain a cheap source of labor. But in the final analysis, the bureau gradually squashed this apprenticing of children, although some black parents themselves did hire out their children for specific and limited periods of time.[29]

Much can be learned from bureau records about the role of the black woman during Reconstruction. With freedom, the status of the black woman changed significantly. Many refused to work in the fields as they once had, and their husbands concurred in this view. Moreover, black women became major contributors to community development through organizing activities and educational work, whether as teachers or simply as concerned parents urging that their children gain some elements of instruction.[30]

Some black women demonstrated great skill in caring for themselves. Emma Hartsfield was living in Austin with Lacy McKenzie, a white man. She stated to the bureau agent that McKenzie had induced her to live with him by promising to give her a house and a lot. After living with him for more than a year, Hartsfield became pregnant and McKenzie proposed that she have an abortion. When Hartsfield refused, McKenzie became angry and threatened to sell the house and lot, throw her out, and leave. She complained of her situation to J.P. Richardson, the Austin agent, and he immediately procured a lawyer to attach the land and "to try and frighten him into a settlement." Shortly thereafter, McKenzie came to the bureau office with Hartsfield and executed a deed to her for lot number eight in Austin with two houses. In return, she "signed an agreement releasing him from all claims." The agent's only comment after all this had transpired was: "Pretty dear pay for one year's _____." (The line is his.)[31]

The involvement of the black community in the political process beginning in 1867 is well documented in the bureau materials. The participation of the bureau in politics varied from state to state and from agent to agent, but in all states, agents were intimately involved in registering black males to vote. In Texas, the bureau regularly reported the number of blacks and whites registered by the registration boards; the statistics from these boards provide a basis for comparison with the percentages of blacks who actually voted. At times the agents also formed Union or Loyal Leagues to encourage blacks to vote for the Republican party. Blacks themselves soon became aware of the power of the vote and also learned the consequences of voting as whites forced blacks to respect the white view of the power structure.[32]

But this is just what the records reveal superficially. On the local level, agents often identified community leaders and their background or occupation. In Millican, Texas, a small community eighty miles northwest of Houston, there was a confrontation between blacks and whites in 1868 as a result of some Ku Klux Klan depredations. The leader of Millican's black community, George E. Brooks, was a preacher, registrar, and member of the Union League. He was not killed in the initial clash, but his second in command, Harry Thomas, was.

Brooks did not, however, escape white retaliation; some days later his decomposed body was found, identifiable only by certain articles of clothing, a pencil, a knife, and a portion of a familiar finger missing from his right hand. Thus, local black leaders led a precarious existence, and a study of communities across the South may reveal a pattern. By killing or running out the black leadership, whites fomented disorganization and instability in the black community and were thereby able to control it more effectively. It might also be surmised that the reason more prominent black leaders did not emerge from the Reconstruction experience is that they were effectively silenced, just as George E. Brooks had been in Millican.[33] Whites all over the South sensed the importance of black leadership; violence was discriminating and purposeful, not random.

From the beginning of Reconstruction, violence was effectively used by whites against blacks. The outrages ranged the whole gamut of the imaginable and unimaginable. At times blacks responded in kind by, for example, firing on and running off a group of Ku Klux Klan members. These retaliations were rare, however, and the black community in general suffered heavily from white incursions. Although violence against blacks usually peaked around election times in an obvious effort to keep blacks from the polls, it was ever present and a constant reminder to blacks of their position in the social structure. The bureau records in Texas, as in other states, are filled with evidence of the breakdown of "law and order" in southern communities in the years after the Civil War.[34] A systematic analysis of this criminal activity is sorely needed, and only then will we fully comprehend its toll on the black community.

The problem of violence was but an adjunct of the larger concern about race relations. When a county bureau agent wrote his monthly report, he was asked to comment on the disposition of the races. So, in Texas at least, race relations can be analyzed on an almost county by county basis over a span of three or four years. Even in a sprawling frontier society, with few inherent social sanctions, race relations did vary from area to area. Much of course depended upon how strongly blacks defended their rights and what percentage of the population they comprised. Areas where blacks equaled or outnumbered whites were scenes of more violence and strained race relations. In a county where whites predominated, overt violence was not necessary.[35]

Bureau records provide glimpses of other aspects of black life. The emergence of an internal structure, for example, in the black community can be seen through bureau records. Through self-organization and supportive institutions, blacks tried to organize and strengthen their efforts to combat white influence and encroachment. Familial ties, religion, and cooperative land buying were all attempts by the freedmen's community to ensure its survival and culture. When bureau agents dealt with the freedpeople they often had to go through the community structure, especially in matters of education, politics, and violence. Letters from blacks themselves to the bureau, or their complaints, give brief insights into black life that are not available in other sources.[36]

Although in the 1860s Texas was predominantly an agricultural society, there were some towns that were experiencing rapid growth and would eventually become part of the urban environment. Places like Galveston, Houston, Austin, and Dallas had a certain urban aura about them that made life for blacks in those areas markedly unlike that of the large segment who were mainly agricultural laborers. Many of the freedpeople in these towns worked for wages and in more skilled positions than the freedpeople in the countryside. Here again, bureau manuscripts do not provide a full view of urban life, but they do give indications of where and how blacks lived, what jobs they were performing, how much property they held, and how they related to the white community. It is, of course, imperative that other sources be consulted to supplement those of the bureau when researching these topics, but the bureau records do provide a beginning.[37]

A feature of keen interest in the Texas situation is that one of the bureau's few black agents, George T. Ruby, was assigned to Galveston. Ruby served the bureau as a teacher and an inspector, and became a delegate to the 1868 state constitutional convention, and ultimately a state legislator. He was very active in bureau affairs before turning to politics. As an inspector, he checked on whether white agents were filling their positions effectively. For example, in evaluating the progress and potential of Edward Miller, an agent for Brazos, Grimes, and part of Burleson counties, Ruby stated:

> He spoke to me of the multiplicity of his duties and of his wish to be transferred to some field where he would have less labor and care. He impressed me (I saw him transact business subsequently) as an earnest officer who would do all he could but who rather lacks the ''savoir faire'' in execution. The freedmen have more or less complaints against him and allege, the more thoughtful ones, as cause for the Captain's conduct that murder was so rampant the S.A.C. [sub-assistant commissioner] dared not act as he should. This Sub District is an exceedingly rough one and nearly as bad as I found at Robertson County.[38]

Then Ruby indicated what was required: ''The people need a little rough handling and this I do not believe Cap't M. can do. . . . At this point, if I may be permitted the suggestion, there is needed an *energetic, faithful* officer who can and will materially aid in the work of 'Reconstruction.' ''[39]

The desire to attain land and education, the two overriding aspirations of blacks early in Reconstruction, appears regularly in the Freedmen's Bureau records. Although blacks hoped they would receive land in a redistribution of properties, this never occurred, for numerous reasons. There were almost no abandoned lands in Texas, so in this respect the bureau was able to do very little. A very small percentage of freedmen were able to purchase land in the towns and in agricultural areas, and a few did acquire property through estates or through the efforts of the bureau, as did the black woman in Austin. These were rare occurrences. The bureau, however, sought to protect those blacks who did own or lease property from unscrupulous whites who tried to divest them of it. With regard to black ownership of property generally, though, the bureau provides only a starting place for research and analysis.[40]

Perhaps the major source of information in bureau records concerning the first years of Reconstruction is in the sphere of black education. Providing educational opportunities was undoubtedly the prime achievement of the bureau. In establishing freedmen's schools throughout the South, and encouraging the black community to take an active part, the bureau put the former bondsmen on the road to literacy. Every state bureau had a superintendent of education and in their records one can find a mine of information. Supplementing bureau educational sources with the American Missionary Association papers gives a fairly complete perspective on the type and length of schooling the freedpeople received. Blacks themselves actively demanded education and worked to establish and support their own schools. Often they pressured the bureau and missionary groups to provide schools in the face of white opposition.

Bureau agents were required to provide monthly reports on the status of education in their respective districts. These reports noted who the teachers were and their color, where the school was located, by whom the teachers were paid, and how many pupils were enrolled in day, night, and Sunday schools. In the superintendent's records, there are figures on how much each state bureau spent to build and maintain schools, lists of teachers, and monthly reports listing the total number of pupils attending both bureau and private schools in the whole state. These listings are not always complete because, at times, the private schoolteachers did not report, but they are about the only records available.

In establishing black schools, the bureau in Texas tried to insulate them forever against the white community. Before a building was repaired or a new one built, the agent usually called a meeting of the black citizens and either made sure they owned the lot on which the structure to be repaired was located, or else had them raise money and purchase a piece of property so that a new school could be erected. The land was owned by a board of trustees who were responsible to the black community. In this way, the bureau attempted to ensure that the schools would always be in the hands of blacks themselves. There were many problems with finding whites who would sell land and assist in the matter of financing, but in a surprising number of cases, through the perseverence of the freedpeople and the bureau, success was attained.

For blacks, attaining an education was one of the many hardships during Reconstruction. Many, if not most, whites were hostile toward bureau efforts to provide schooling for blacks, and they retaliated with such overt acts of violence as burning schoolhouses and assaulting teachers, both black and white. And black financial difficulties did not help to maintain a stable system. Freedmen's education was directly tied to their economic situation. If the crops were plentiful, then they could afford to pay a small amount of tuition, if necessary, so that a teacher could be paid. As one agent wrote in Houston in 1867, the "freedpeople are deeply solicitous upon the education of themselves and [their] children, but are too poor, owing to the failure of the cotton crop, being unable to obtain work, they are barely able to earn sufficient to procure the actual necessaries of life." Civil authorities were not disposed to aid them. Like many other bureau personnel, the agent believed that unless teachers were maintained by the government and suitable buildings furnished, little progress would be made in advancing the cause of education. This was true not only for Houston and the state generally, but all over the South as well.[41]

While all the possibilities for using Freedmen's Bureau records have by no means been indicated in this paper, a brief summary of bureau holdings may be helpful. The records of the bureau include significant materials on the black community in relation to education, labor, politics, crime, migration, families, adjustment to freedom, race relations, and community structure. There is less on housing, urban life and occupations, medical care, property ownership, social structure, and internal divisions within the black community itself. This should not deter any researcher, however, for the glimpses that are provided raise questions, and will hopefully lead to an intensive search for supplementary materials to gain a composite picture of what life was like for the black masses during those first momentous years of freedom.

The quantity of bureau records varies from state to state. The Texas records form a medium-sized collection, comprising around 173 bound volumes of varying length, and 44 boxes of manuscripts. Some state collections are smaller, but several are much larger and contain more complete records, especially on such topics as medical care, which is barely touched upon in the Texas bureau records.

Some Freedmen's Bureau records are available in National Archives depositories around the country. Now in progress is a comprehensive microfilm production of the bureau materials, with attendant microcopy pamphlets. Those records already prepared, or in progress, are those of the commissioner's office for Georgia, Alabama, Mississippi, South Carolina, North Carolina, and Texas.[42] It is hoped that in the future these microfilms will be distributed to the various federal records centers around the country so that historians everywhere may use them. At present they may be obtained only by purchase and cannot be sent out on interlibrary loan.

One caveat concerning the microfilm is in order. The bureau records being filmed relate only to the assistant commissioners' or national commissioner's offices; in addition, they include the records of the quartermaster and disbursing officer, and the records of the superintendents of education. There can be no doubt that these records are immensely valuable. The most penetrating insights into black life, however, are to be found in the materials of the local agents. Many of these manuscripts, such as letters to and from local blacks and whites, are not duplicated in the headquarters' records, and therefore may be consulted only in the National Archives building. Without these manuscripts, the historians will lose much of what was going on in community after community in the South after the war; this is where the bureau records have been slighted the most.

The Freedmen's Bureau records have only begun to be tapped for the tremendous amount of materials that awaits those seriously interested in black history. In order to begin to understand what went on in the South during Reconstruction, notably in the black community, the Records of the Bureau of Refugees, Freedmen, and Abandoned Lands (Record Group 105) are an indispensable starting place.

NOTES

1. James R. Mock, "The National Archives with Respect to the Records of the Negro," *Journal of Negro History* 23 (January 1938): 49-56; Roland C. McConnell, "Importance of Records in the National Archives on the History of the Negro," ibid., 34 (April 1949): 148.

2. David Donald, "Reconstruction," *Interpreting American History: Conversations with Historians,* ed. John A. Garraty, 2 vols. (New York: The Macmillan Co., 1970), 1: 354.

3. The two most recent state studies of the bureau are: Martin Abbott, *The Freedmen's Bureau in South Carolina, 1865-1872* (Chapel Hill: University of North Carolina Press, 1967); Howard A. White, *The Freedmen's Bureau in Louisiana* (Baton Rouge: Louisiana State University Press, 1970). The main problem with these two studies is that they tend to be exclusively administrative instead of social history, and consequently the focus is on the upper echelons at the state level rather than at the local, where the bureau did its most effective work in interacting with blacks. This same difficulty is seen in the older works on the bureau. For a listing of the earlier books on the bureau, see Barry A. Crouch, "The Freedmen's Bureau in Texas: A Reevaluation" (ms.). See also, the author's critique of White's study in *Societas: A Review of Social History* 1 (Autumn 1971): 317-18. On the national level, William S. McFeely has made some controversial suggestions about bureau hindrance of black aspirations, but the book is marred by poor research, and almost no research was done in the local agents' materials. McFeely, *Yankee Stepfather: General O.O. Howard and the Freedmen* (New Haven and London: Yale University Press, 1968); and, "Unfinished Business: The Freedmen's Bureau and Federal Action in Race Relations," *Key Issues in the Afro-American Experience,* eds. Nathan I. Huggins, Martin Kilson, and Daniel M. Fox, *et al.* 2 vols. (New York: Harcourt Brace Jovanovich, 1971), 2: 5-25. An opposing view is presented in, John A. Carpenter, *Sword and Olive Branch: Oliver Otis Howard* (Pittsburgh: University of Pittsburgh Press, 1964).

4. Present studies include, John W. Blassingame, *The Slave Community: Plantation Life in the Antebellum South* (New York, London, and Toronto: Oxford University Press, 1972); Stanley Feldstein, *Once A Slave: The Slaves' View of Slavery* (New York: William Morrow and Co., 1971). C. Vann Woodward, in the Fourth Annual Rayford W. Logan Lecture at Howard University, discussed the possibilities of the slave narratives as valid sources for recounting the slave's life, and stated that Eugene D. Genovese, "who has written an account of slave religion, is the first serious historian of slavery to make full use of the WPA and Fisk narrative collections," *Washington Post,* 30 April 1973, p. B-2.

5. My own work and the following pages will, hopefully, make these assertions abundantly clear. Prof. Herbert Gutman and a number of his students are currently pursuing studies which reveal much about black behavior and culture. The author is especially indebted to Leslie R. Lowrey and John O'Brien. The slave culture is recounted in Blassingame, *The Slave Community.* A recent work that partially extends these ideas into the Reconstruction period is, Joel Williamson, *After Slavery: The Negro in South Carolina during Reconstruction, 1861-1877* (Chapel Hill: University of North Carolina Press, 1965).

6. James P. Flint to H.A. McCaleb (Bureau Superintendent, Louisville), 8 September 1865, Assistant Commissioner (AC), Letters Received (LR), 1865, M-83, Tennessee and Kentucky, Bureau of Refugees, Freedmen, and Abandoned Lands, Record Group 105, National Archives Building; J.C. Randolph (Nicholasville, Kentucky) to Oliver Otis Howard, 11 September 1865, AC, LR, R-25, ibid. (Unless otherwise indicated all citations will be to the bureau records, and will be identified only by state.)

7. Almost all the assistant commissioner, letters received files, have any number of letters from whites concerning this particular phenomenon. For various myths surrounding the freedmen and their freedom, see McFeely, "The Hidden Freedmen: Five Myths in the Reconstruction Era," *The Black Experience in America: Selected Essays,* eds. James C. Curtis and Lewis L. Gould (Austin and London: University of Texas Press, 1970), pp. 68-86.

8. Chauncey C. Morse to the Assistant Commissioner of Louisiana, 15 September 1865, Texas, vol. 4, p. 3; Edgar M. Gregory (Assistant Commissioner, Texas) to Rufus Saxton (Assistant Commissioner, Georgia), 19 September 1865, ibid., p. 5; Gregory to Messers and Brothers Helman, 30 October, 1865, ibid., p. 36. These are but three examples; there are countless others in all levels of the records.

9. Bell Irvin Wiley, *Southern Negroes, 1861-1865* (New Haven: Yale University Press, 1938), p. 5; James Arthur Lyon Fremantle, *The Fremantle Diary,* ed. and comp. Walter Lord (Boston: Little, Brown, & Co., 1954), pp. 63-64. A good indication of how many slaves were brought into Texas is that Gregory reported there were 400,000 blacks in early 1866, Gregory to Oliver Otis Howard, 31 January 1866, Texas, vol. 4, p. 123. The 1870 census listed only 253,475.

10. Thomas W. Conway to William Fowler (Assistant Adjutant General, Washington), 7 August 1865, AC, Letters Sent, Louisiana, vol. 15, p. 232; Fowler to Conway, 5 October 1865, AC, LR, ibid., R-228, Box 6; J.C. DeGress to John S. Imboden, 31 October 1865, Texas, vol. 100, p. 13.

11. The early letters of Edgar M. Gregory to Oliver Otis Howard, in vol. 4, Texas, reveals this quite clearly.

12. J.C. DeGress to Captain Wardlow (Commanding Detachment, 12th Ill. Cav.), 3 November 1865, Texas, vol. 100, pp. 18-19.

13. W.R. Stickney (Assistant Superintendent of Freedmen, Shreveport) to Thomas W. Conway, 1 August 1865, AC, LR, Louisiana, S-68, Box 6.

14. The most suggestive work in this area is, J. Thomas May, "The Medical Care of Blacks in Louisiana during Occupation and Reconstruction, 1862-1868: Its Social and Political Background" (Ph.D. diss., Department of History, Tulane University, 1970). The author is indebted to Professor May for many of the ideas in the following paragraphs.

15. Ibid.

16. Ibid. For those blacks sent to Texas see, letters received by the assistant commissioner of South Carolina. On Charles Griffin's death, Charles Garretson to Oliver Otis Howard, 15 September 1867, Texas, vol. 5, p. 145.

17. References to health care are scattered throughout the Texas Bureau records, and this paragraph is a brief summary of those references.

18. May, "The Medical Care of Blacks in Louisiana," *passim;* Alan Raphael, "Health and Social Welfare of Kentucky Black People, 1865-1870," *Societas* 2 (Spring 1972): 143-57. Volume 173 of the Texas records is some type of hospital admissions record, but it is very sketchy and incomplete.

19. William H. Sinclair to Chauncey C. Morse, 9 March 1866, Texas, vol. 4, p. 157, and many other references scattered throughout the Texas Bureau materials.

20. William H. Sinclair (Inspector) to J.T. Kirkman, 26 February 1867, Texas, Box 21. Sinclair's report was attached to the letter.

21. Ibid.

22. Ibid.

23. Ibid.

24. Ibid.

25. Ibid. See also, J.W. Throckmorton (Governor) to James Oakes (Agent, Austin), 18 March 1867, Texas, vol. 46. (Some of the Texas volumes do not have page numbers).

26. M.E. Davis (Agent, Houston) to Charles Vernou, 31 July 1868, Texas, vol. 103, p. 142. There are forty-four volumes in the Texas local records that deal with complaints.

27. J.P. Richardson, Journal, 11 July 1867, Texas, vol. 52, p. 20.

28. The Texas records are simply filled with these types of requests. On the local level see, Crouch, "The Freedmen's Bureau and the 30th Sub-District in Texas: Smith County

and Its Environs during Reconstruction,'' *Chronicles of Smith County, Texas* 11 (Spring 1972): 15-30.

29. Ibid.

30. The Texas bureau materials contain a surprising amount on black women and their role during Reconstruction. The author is in the process of preparing a manuscript on this subject.

31. J.P. Richardson, Journal, 6 July 1867; Texas, vol. 52, p. 15.

32. Volumes 46 through 172 contain the local Texas records, and here the political materials can be found.

33. N.H. Randlett (Agent, Bryan) to Charles Vernou, 23 July 1868, AC, LR, Texas, R-21, Box 9. The author has almost completed a manuscript on this event, from which these two paragraphs are excerpted, entitled: "Affair At Millican: The Freedmen's Bureau, a Black Community, and Race Relations in Texas."

34. The violence in Texas during Reconstruction was truly staggering. Besides the operations reports of the local agents in boxes 13-19, see Criminal Offenses Committed in the State of Texas, AC, Austin, volumes 11-13. The army records contain additional materials on outrages.

35. Ibid.

36. For but one example, see the indenture made by Edward Capps for the Colored Cavalry Association when they rented a building to the bureau for school purposes, August 14, 1867, Box 42. The records of the local agents abound with these references.

37. The local records for Galveston, Houston, Austin, and Dallas, provide numerous insights into black town life.

38. G.T. Ruby (Inspector) to J.T. Kirkman, 23 June 1867, AC, LR, Texas, R-186, Box 4.

39. Ibid.

40. One example is the attempt by the bureau to protect the rights of Samuel Pointer who had a twenty-year lease on some land in Houston. Two white men sold the land while the lease was still in effect. W.B. Pease (Agent, Houston) to Abner Doubleday (Agent, Galveston), 11 March 1867, Texas, Box 42.

41. M.E. Davis (Agent, Houston) to J.P. Richardson, 2 December 1867, Texas, vol. 103, p. 18. The other observations about education are gleaned from, volumes 3 and 6, 14-23, and the reports of the local agents.

42. The following pamphlets, all published by the National Archives, are listed with their microcopy numbers: Elaine Everly, comp., *Preliminary Inventory of the Records of the Bureau of Refugees, Freedmen, and Abandoned Lands, Washington Headquarters* (1973), PI-174; *Selected Series of Records Issued by the Commissioner of the Bureau of Refugees, Freedmen, and Abandoned Lands, 1865-1872* (1969), M-742; *Registers and Letters Received by the Commissioner of the Bureau of Refugees, Freedmen, and Abandoned Lands, 1865-1872* (1973), M-752; *Records of the Assistant Commissioner for the State of Georgia, Bureau of Refugees, Freedmen, and Abandoned Lands, 1865-1869* (1969), M-798; *Records of the Superintendent of Education for the State of Georgia, Bureau of Refugees, Freedmen, and Abandoned Lands, 1865-1870* (1969), M-799; *Records of the Education Division of the Bureau of Refugees, Freedmen, and Abandoned Lands, 1865-1871* (1972), M-803; *Records of the Assistant Commissioner for the State of Alabama, Bureau of Refugees, Freedmen, and Abandoned Lands, 1865-1870* (1972), M-809; *Records of the Superintendent of Education for the State of Alabama, Bureau of Refugees, Freedmen, and Abandoned Lands, 1865-1870* (1972), M-810. All the records are, of course, in Record Group 105.

Discussion Summary

A commentator from the floor began the discussion by inquiring about the accessibility of Freedmen's Bureau records and the identification or labeling of materials found therein.

Barry A. Crouch of the University of Maryland reiterated that the Freedmen's Bureau holdings contain a significant amount of material on education, labor, politics, crime, migration, families' adjustments to freedom, race relations, and community affairs/structure. There is less on housing, urban life and occupations, medical care, property ownership, social structure, and internal divisions within the black community itself.

The quality of bureau records, continued Crouch, varies from state to state. The Texas records, for example, form a collection comprising approximately 173 bound volumes, varying in length, and 44 boxes of manuscripts. Other state collections have more complete records and cover such topics as medical care, which is barely touched upon by the Texas bureau.

Crouch commented further on the accessibility of Freedmen's Bureau records. He noted that some bureau records are available to those pursuing research outside the National Archives. Now in progress is a comprehensive microfilm production of the bureau materials, with attendant microcopy pamphlets. Those state collections that have already been filmed, or are in progress, are the records of the commissioner's office for Georgia, Alabama, Mississippi, South Carolina, North Carolina, and Texas. At present, the microfilms are not available on interlibrary loan but may be obtained by purchase.

Crouch was asked to comment on his findings in relationship to a group of slaves who organized an emancipation camp in Houston, Texas. He said that he was not aware of such a group, although he had discovered a group in Galveston, Texas, called the Colored Cavalry Association that owned a building that they later rented to the bureau to set up a school. This, he thought, indicated self-organization and obviously property ownership.

Carleton Hayden of Howard University was concerned about land acquisition by freedwomen and men. He wondered if local agents had kept records on land purchases. Crouch replied that the two overriding aspirations of blacks for land and education early in Reconstruction appear regularly in the Freedmen's Bureau records. These records are valuable in that they list the organization and membership of land acquisition. For numerous reasons, blacks did not receive land in a redistribution. There were almost no abandoned lands in Texas; therefore, the bureau was able to do very little. A small percentage of freedpeople were able to purchase land in towns and agricultural areas. A few acquired property through estates or through the efforts of the bureau. Alabama and Mississippi had extensive land acquisition programs, but the Texas program was not as progressive.

A conference participant raised the question: What were the attitudes of the bureau officials in terms of understanding the plight of blacks? In response, Crouch mentioned John H. Sinclair, the bureau official who inspected the state penitentiary. He was obviously sympathetic to blacks, since he was involved in the bureau program during the whole time it existed in Texas. Crouch concluded that one has to read between lines in order to know whether an agent was really interested in protecting the black community. If any violence occurred, the agent usually called in the troops to negotiate in some way with the white community. In some instances, however, when agents were sympathetic to blacks, they were killed.

With reference to Crouch's extensive analysis of blacks serving terms in the Huntsville prison, the question was raised: What were the minimum/maximum sentences in relationship to the harshness of crimes committed? Crouch replied that the average sentences were three years and sixty-four days.

A conference participant was interested in Crouch's statement concerning what he outlined to be the greatest expertise of black women. Crouch said that he had attempted to point out very briefly that black women were community leaders, not only in educational projects, but in other projects as well; however, he could not detail them. He said that his comment about black women moving into the house after slavery was not meant to be offensive. Even though the change was simplistic, it was a highly significant one because, after all, during slavery black women worked in the fields and had no time to tend their children or deal with family matters or social concerns.

Lucille Bridges of the Division of Instructional Television, Maryland State Department of Education, Baltimore, noted that there was a disparity between the number of black women and men serving terms in prisons. She questioned whether that comparison reflected an attitude on the part of authorities that perhaps the black woman might have been less dangerous and, therefore, was able to exert a little more leadership in the community. Crouch said he realized the disparity, but he thought it was highly significant that there were fourteen black women and no white women serving terms in prisons. He said this indicated that black women were active.

In concluding the discussion, Crouch emphasized that both black women and men were punished for trivial crimes committed. Rose Moore of Upshur County, for instance, served two years for allegedly stealing a pig. In another case, Judy Hammer of Coryell County received two years on a burglary charge. Elvira Mays served two years for giving her husband a pickaxe so he could escape jail, and Georgia Swanson received the same sentence for allegedly stealing a night gown. And these were only a few of the examples in which blacks were punished for such trivial crimes.

IV

Related Records and Projects

Presidential Libraries as Sources for Research on Afro-Americans

J. C. JAMES

When researchers begin to think of the presidential libraries as a part of the federal establishment, they are baffled by the fact that as institutions the presidential libraries do not have much history. Yet, in spite of their lack of history, they have become a significant factor in the search for our identity as a nation and as a people.

The Franklin D. Roosevelt Library is the first and oldest of the six libraries that make up the presidential library system. It all began when President Roosevelt offered to the American people his public papers, many of his private papers, his huge personal library of some fifteen hundred volumes, and his famous model ship collection, along with thousands of other museum items and art objects. In addition, he gave sixteen acres of his ancestral estate along the Hudson at Hyde Park, New York, for the construction of the edifice which today houses not only his papers, but the papers of Eleanor Roosevelt and dozens of their associates in public and private life.

Since 1939, when Congress accepted this generous offer via a joint resolution, the Roosevelt Library has maintained one of the most unique and valuable collections of extant research materials. Today it ranks number three among centers for research in American history. Franklin D. Roosevelt has now surpassed Abraham Lincoln as the American most written about. The Franklin D. Roosevelt Library has been used as the background and prototype for other presidential libraries that have followed.

In examining the libraries' holdings as sources for research in Afro-American history, one should consider them in the order of presidential administrations rather than in the order of establishment. This paper is simply an effort to guide researchers to sources that may prove rewarding in their search for the true meaning of the black experience in America. In most instances, documents specifically mentioned in this paper are but a sampling of the millions of items awaiting exploration.

The Herbert Hoover Library
West Branch, Iowa

In 1929, which now seems like antiquity, when they were considered at all, the problems of Afro-Americans were referred to as the "Colored Question." One of the hottest controversies of that year raged around Mrs. Oscar DePriest, the wife of the newly elected black congressman from Chicago, who had the audacity to present herself at the White House for a tea to which all the wives and families of congressmen had been invited. There are two archives containers among the presidential papers that are devoted entirely to the reactions of white America, particularly white America below the Mason-Dixon line. The southern press was scandalized, southern congressmen were outraged, and southern legislatures passed resolutions condemning social equality as symbolized by her attendance at this function. Correspondence, newspaper clippings, and copies of resolutions are the chief materials in the presidential library regarding that incident.

Hoover served as secretary of the Commerce Department from 1921 to 1928. The documents generated during his appointment to Commerce relate to colored clerks in the Bureau of the Census, colored industries, Mississippi flood relief work for blacks, and unemployment among blacks. The presidential papers subject file contains information about appointments, lynchings, segregation, and discrimination, the Judge Parker (John J.) nomination, and the Negro Industrial Commission. In the files of the president's secretary are significant documents relating to organizations and individuals, including the NAACP, National Negro Bankers League, National Negro Bankers Association, Colored Farmers Bureau. Other noteworthy files contain information on Robert S. Abbott, Will W. Alexander, Senator Coleman (Cole) Blease, Col. B.O. Davis, W.E.B. Du

Bois, John R. Hawkins, T. Arnold Hill, Charles S. Johnson, and Walter White. In the presidential personal files, one can find evidence that reflects some awareness of black educational and civic activities. For example, there are materials on Lincoln University (Pennsylvania), Tuskegee Institute, Fisk University, Howard University, Hampton Institute, the National Negro Insurance Association, Committee on Interracial Cooperation, Wilberforce University, Atlanta University, Meharry Medical College, the Rockefeller and Rosenwald Foundations, Mary McLeod Bethune, the Rev. A. Clayton Powell, Sr., and black women's clubs. All of these organizations and individuals were guideposts and benchmarks and almost always looked upon as spokespersons or representatives of blacks.

The presidential subject file contains materials on black army regiments, including the correspondence of Herbert Hoover, Douglas MacArthur, Oscar DePriest, and Robert R. Moton regarding the suspension of enlistments and promotions in black regiments and the transfer of the Tenth Cavalry to northern stations.

Blacks involvement in foreign affairs was practically nonexistent, except for the limited contacts with Haiti and Liberia. However, a check of the materials on black appointments might reveal an occasional black appointment to a consular post in other parts of the world.

The Franklin D. Roosevelt Library
Hyde Park, New York

The New Deal of Franklin D. Roosevelt was much more than a slogan. For millions of Americans, including blacks, there was indeed a new deal—a radical departure from the past in attitude and deed. Roosevelt appeared not to shrink from his responsibilities as president of all the people. He showed genuine concern for the plight of the ill-fed, the ill-clothed, and the ill-housed; and he was not afraid to be seen with a black woman or man in a professional or social relationship. In other words, blacks began to enjoy visibility in high places, to glimpse and feel the excitement of power though still far from its sources.

Perhaps the most important files among presidential papers in the Roosevelt Library dealing with blacks are the official file and the president's personal file. The official file contains the largest single body of materials relating to lynching, segregation, and race riots during that administration. Among the files on several government agencies are papers relating chiefly to the employment of blacks. Files of agencies containing substantial amounts of materials on blacks include the Civil Service Commission, Veterans Administration, U.S. Post Office, Civilian Conservation Corps, Federal Emergency Relief Administration, and the departments of Agriculture, Commerce, Interior, Labor, State, and War. Official file 300 (the Democratic National Committee) contains a great deal of correspondence from southern states relating to blacks.

The president's personal file provides a relatively complete breakdown of black organizations, the channels through which blacks articulated their aspirations and frustrations. Aside from the files on the NAACP and the Urban League, there are sizeable files on the Association for the Study of Negro Life and History, Colored National Democratic League, Negro Newspaper Publishers Association, and the National Association of Teachers. Files relating to individuals contain information on Judge William H. Hastie, Edgar G. Brown, and Mary McLeod Bethune.

The papers of Eleanor Roosevelt contain correspondence with prominent blacks: namely, Mary McLeod Bethune, Crystal Bird Fauset, Elder Solomon Lightfoot Michaux, A. Philip Randolph, Walter White, and Roy Wilkins. Other important papers relating to blacks in the Franklin D. Roosevelt Library include those of Aubrey Williams, executive director of National Youth Administration; Leon Henderson, Office of Price Administration (OPA) administrator; Lowell Mellett, administrative assistant to the president; and John Carmody, administrator of the Rural Electrification Administration.

The file on the Democratic National Committee does not have any separate correspondence that relate to blacks specifically, but among its states files, there is scattered documentation, especially from the southern states. Also included are records on the Women's Division of the Democratic National Committee covering relations with the Colored Voters Division from 1933 to 1936. The large number of photographs of blacks among the approximately one hundred thousand photographs in the audiovisual collection at the library provides an important visual link in the study of the black experience during the Roosevelt years. Although the collection contains a variety and an abundance of materials concerning blacks, there are significant gaps. One such example is the absence of important information concerning the Black Cabinet. This term was applied to the relatively large number of well-educated, sophisticated, and experienced blacks that were brought to Washington in the early days of the New Deal to serve in high ranking positions as bona fide presidential appointees, and, as John Hope Franklin puts it, "oathbound servants of the United States." They were the "Black Brain Trust," a group worthy of recognition in any setting. Most went on to later and greater achievements and fame. The Black Cabinet included Robert L. Vann, editor of the *Pittsburgh Courier,* who served as a special assistant to the attorney general; William H. Hastie, dean of the Howard University Law School, who was appointed assistant solicitor in the Department of Interior and who went on to become civilian aide to the secretary of war and the first black judge to serve on a federal circuit court; Robert C. Weaver, who became the first racial adviser in the Department of Interior, and who later became the first black member of a president's cabinet as secretary of Housing and Urban Development under President Johnson; and Mary McLeod Bethune, who served as director of the National Youth Administration. Unfortunately, the papers of none of the persons identified as members of the Black Cabinet have been deposited in the Franklin D. Roosevelt Library.

The Roosevelt era remains one of the most fascinating and fruitful periods for research and inquiry in American history. It has already proved so for political, social, and economic research on America as a whole. As for research relating to Afro-Americans based on archival sources, we have just begun. Appendix A, which follows this paper, is a list of articles relating to blacks based in part on sources in the Roosevelt Library.

The Harry S. Truman Library
Independence, Missouri

In examining the records of the presidential libraries, one becomes aware of a certain sameness among people and organizations, and the problems with which they cope. The collections in all the presidential libraries contain extensive files on presidential and departmental dealings with the NAACP, the Urban League, discrimination in jobs, education, housing, and voting rights. During each administration, a few developments—both positive and negative—stand out for Afro-Americans. During the Truman years, these developments were the president's Committee on Equality of Treatment and Opportunity in the U.S. Armed Services and the president's Committee on Civil Rights.

The president's Committee on Civil Rights was established by Executive Order 9808, December 5, 1946, for the purpose of recommending ways to strengthen the capability of federal, state, and local laws to safeguard the civil rights of all the people. The committee's records (1946-1947) consist of general correspondence and administrative records, correspondence with government agencies, individuals, institutions, and organizations.

Also included are records of meetings and hearings, staff interviews, statements of witnesses, staff memorandums and recommendations, reference files, and reports. Of particular interest are the files on lynching, District of Columbia problems (including the National Theater), the Civil Rights Division of the Department of Justice, the Civil Service Commission, and the Veterans Administration.

Correspondence concerning several individuals may prove most informative. Among them are Will Alexander, Chester Bowles, Tom Clark, Charles H. Houston, Langston Hughes, Harold Ickes, V.O. Key, Eleanor Roosevelt, and Louis Wright, to name just a few. The president's Committee on Equality of Treatment and Opportunity in the U.S. Armed Services was established by Executive Order 9981, July 26, 1948. Its mission was to determine ways to improve the operations of the armed services and thereby insure equality of treatment and opportunity for all members of the U.S. Armed Services without regard to race, color, religion, or national origin. The chairperson of that committee was Charles Fahy.

The general files of the committee consist of general correspondence, records of meetings, reports, memorandums, publications, newspaper clippings, and other related materials. Of special interest is the schedule indicating meetings with the president, secretary of the army Gordon Gray, and Gen. Omar Bradley. These sessions were held at Fort Knox, Fort Bragg, in New York City and Leyte, Philippines.

The president's Committee on Equality of Treatment and Opportunity also maintains a separate series of correspondence for each branch of the armed forces. For example, the air force files contain reports and correspondence that relate to visits to air force installations, the redistribution of black personnel, and statistical reports on the number of black personnel. The army records contain materials on Army General Classification Test (AGCT) scores, enlistments and distribution of black troops, career field charts, enlistment qualifications, black platoons in white companies, West Point, and recommendations for army action. The navy records contain files on Annapolis, black officers, and the steward's branch.

In addition, the Truman Library has nineteen volumes of transcripts of committee hearings, a very extensive file of newspaper clippings, and a small body of classified materials. Researchers who wish to gain access to this material should seek the guidance of the archivist responsible for this collection.

Other collections in the Truman Library that may be of interest are the papers of Philleo Nash, administrative assistant to the president, with special responsibility for those activities related to the Fair Employment Practices Commission (FEPC), and the desegregation of the U.S. Armed Services. The papers of Stephen J. Spingarn, a member of the White House staff, and those of Francis P. Matthews, a member of the president's Committee on Civil Rights may also prove useful to a researcher in Afro-American history.

The Dwight D. Eisenhower Library
Abilene, Kansas

The Eisenhower Library holdings reflect or mirror the struggle that exploded in the streets of the nation during the sixties. There is a noticeable increase in civil rights activity and documentation. Approximately 107,000 pages of materials related to blacks and civil rights can be found throughout the files of the White House and government agencies of the Eisenhower administration. Important subjects covered in the central files are employment, the Civil Rights Act of 1957 and the Commission on Civil Rights created by the act, black suffrage, school desegregation, including 2,000 pages of materials relating to incidents in Little Rock, Arkansas. Additional files on school desegregation and the Little Rock situation are included in what is described as bulk mail files of low-level public correspondence. These contain some 45,000 pages. Also of special interest are the library's holdings relating to the *Brown* decision of 1954.

Other collections, including the so-called staff files, are those of Alvan C. Gillem, Jr. relating to the Gillem Board report on blacks in the U.S. Armed Services, David W. Kendall relating to black suffrage, James P. Mitchell on nondiscrimination in employment, Gerald D. Morgan relating to the Civil Rights Commission, and William P. Rogers on the Civil Rights Act of 1957.

The highest ranking black appointee of the Eisenhower administration was E. Frederick Morrow, who was a White House administrative officer for special projects. Three separate groups of Morrow's papers are preserved in the library. Also included in the Morrow files is a considerable volume of materials on other black leaders.

Finally, though small (only fifty pages), the file labeled "DDE's [Dwight D. Eisenhower's] Attitude Toward Blacks" should prove particularly fascinating.

The John F. Kennedy Library
Waltham, Massachusetts

Most of the records in the Kennedy Library are still being processed; therefore, it is difficult to pinpoint materials relating to Afro-Americans and civil rights except through governmental activity and agencies known to have been involved in the struggle for equality during the period.

Of the general records produced by the Kennedy administration and now in the Kennedy Library are the White House office files and the White House central files, which are certain to prove productive if approached with specific subjects in mind. There are 123 rolls of microfilm from the Civil Rights Division of the Department of Justice and 91 rolls from the Civil Rights Commission.

The Kennedy Library holdings also contain the papers of Robert F. Kennedy (including the Senate and Department of Justice years), Burke Marshall, Lee White, and Harris Wofford, White House aides, and microfilmed records of civil rights activities of various departments and agencies.

The personal papers of other individuals in the Kennedy administration who were involved in civil rights include those of Berl Bernhard, Ted Sorensen, Meyer Feldman, Arthur Schlesinger, Jr., Pedro San Juan, Abraham Ribicoff, and Adam Yarmolinsky.

The Kennedy Library, in spite of its limited operations, has already made a considerable contribution in the area of oral history. The library has several hundred recorded interviews pertaining to civil rights. A sampling reveals interviews with such interesting and well-known individuals as Ross Barnett, Berl Bernhard, Simeon Booker, Emanuel Cellar, Ramsey Clark, Justice William O. Douglas, James Farmer, Orville Faubus, Aaron Henry, Pedro San Juan, Robert Kennedy, Martin Luther King, Jr., Nicholas Katzenbach, Marjorie and Belford Lawson, Burke Marshall, Thurgood Marshall, Ralph McGill, Clarence Mitchell, A. Philip Randolph, Joe Rauh, Hobart Taylor, George Wallace, Robert Weaver, and Roy Wilkins.

For the researcher interested in the United States' relations with Africa, the files of McGeorge Bundy, special assistant for National Security Affairs, include a series on countries. There is a similar series in the president's office files that were maintained by Evelyn Lincoln. This file contains valuable correspondence between the president and African heads of states. Unfortunately, however, these records are still under security classification.

The Lyndon B. Johnson Library
Austin, Texas

President Lyndon B. Johnson expressed the wish to be known as the "education president." Certainly he demonstrated a concern and provided the momentum for the most extensive and far-reaching educational programs at the federal level to-date. In fact, what took place in the field of education during the Johnson administration was nothing less than a revolution, and it was not limited to school desegregation, though its achievements in that arena were not inconsiderable. In domestic affairs, the overriding issues of the Johnson years were education and civil rights.

The Johnson Library, established in 1965 and located on the campus of the University of Texas, Austin, is still processing the president's papers and those of many of his associates. Fortunately, the civil rights records are available for research.

The White House central files are organized in broad subject categories and cover virtually every aspect of education and civil rights. These files contain several series of records relating to presidential speeches and messages, including background data, drafts, press releases, and incoming letters of reactions to the messages and speeches. Examples are speeches made at the signing of the Civil Rights Act of 1964 and the Voting Rights Act of 1965.

Other noteworthy series that contain significant materials on Afro-Americans are (1) the Human Rights series, which comprises the records on human and civil rights, including presidential meetings with civil rights leaders, the Civil Rights Act of 1964, black appointees, the 1968 riots that occurred after Martin Luther King's death, employment of blacks in federal agencies, and information on the White House Conference on Equal Opportunity that was held August 9-20, 1965; (2) the Education Schooling series, which contains information on the application of Title I (Compensatory Education) of the Elementary and Secondary Education Act of 1965; (3) the Ideologies series, which includes materials on racial groups and un-American activities as related to blacks and other minorities; (4) the Judicial-Legal series, which contains documentation relating to the assassination of Martin Luther King, Jr.; and (5) the Legislative series, which includes valuable information, from the White House vantage point, on civil rights and education acts. Several files and series deal with legislation, two of which seem particularly significant for our purposes. The "Reports on Legislation" is a file on the status of pending legislation prepared in the form of reports to the president. These were weekly reports originating in the departments or agencies affected by the proposed legislation and routed to the president through Lawrence O'Brien, Barefoot Sanders, and other aides who used them to brief the president prior to his weekly congressional leadership breakfast.

The "Reports to the President on Enrolled Legislation" file, which was prepared by the director of legislative reference, Bureau of the Budget, covers all bills—public and private—and joint resolutions. The reports include statements of purpose, agency recommendations, ramifications, and frequently handwritten notations on the action taken. Attached to each report are congressional committee reports, copies of the final act or resolution, and press releases. Such materials should prove especially interesting and revealing as background on civil rights legislation.

In a speech at Howard University, June 6, 1965, President Johnson announced his intentions to hold a conference on civil rights. In February 1966, he appointed a twenty-nine member council to plan the conference. The council settled on four areas for discussion: economic security and welfare, education, housing, and the administration of justice. The conference was held in Washington, D.C., June 1-2, 1966. Its chairperson was Ben Hieneman, vice chairpersons were Walter E. Fauntroy and Edward C. Sylvester, Jr., and A. Philip Randolph served as honorary chairperson. The report of the conference was issued under the general title, "To Fulfill These Rights."

The records of the Eisenhower Commission (Milton Eisenhower, chairman of the commission) are also in the Johnson Library and are available for research. They contain valuable information on the National Commission on the Causes and Prevention of Violence (NCCPV), the Kerner Commission, and the National Advisory Commission on Civil Disorders.

Finally, the library maintains a file on statements made by President Johnson regarding civil rights, both as vice president and president; a small body of valuable records covering prepresidential years; and the launching of the library's program to facilitate use of oral history.

APPENDIX

Articles Relating to Blacks Based in Part on Sources in the Franklin D. Roosevelt Library

Bain, George W. "How Negro Editors Viewed the New Deal." *Journalism Quarterly* 44 (Autumn 1967): 552-54.

Brewer, James H. "Robert Lee Vann, Democrat or Republican: An Exponent of Loose Leaf Politics." *Negro History Bulletin* 21 (February 1958): 100-103.

Burns, Augustus M. "North Carolina and the Negro Dilemma." *Dissertation Abstracts International* 31 (July 1970): 334A.

*Cantor, Louis. "A Prologue to the Protest Movement: The Missouri Sharecropper Roadside Demonstration of 1939." *Journal of American History* 55 (March 1969): 804-22.

*Capeci, Dominic J., Jr. "The Harlem Riot of 1943." *Dissertation Abstracts International* 31 (April 1971).

Dalfiume, Richard M. "Military Segregation and the 1940 Presidential Election." *Phylon* 30 (Spring 1969): 42-55.

*———. "The 'Forgotten Years' of the Negro Revolution." *Journal of American History* 55 (June 1968): 90-106.

Dunn, Larry W. "Knoxville Negro Voting and the Roosevelt Revolution, 1928-36." *East Tennessee Historical Society's Publications* 43 (1971): 71-93.

Finkle, Lee. "Forum for Protest: The Black Press during World War II." Ph.D. dissertation, New York University, 1971.

Fishel, Leslie. "The Negro in the New Deal Era." *Wisconsin Magazine Historical* 48 (Winter 1964): 111-26.

Gordon, Rita W. "The Change in the Political Alignment of Chicago's Negroes during the New Deal." *Journal of American History* 56 (December 1969): 584-603.

Grant, Robert B. "The Negro Comes to the City: A Documentary History from the Great Migration to the Great Depression." *Dissertation Abstracts International* 32 (December 1971): 3205A.

Harrell, James A. "Negro Leadership in the Election Year 1936." *Journal of Southern History* 34 (November 1968): 546-64.

*Kifer, Allen F. "The Negro Under the New Deal, 1933-41." *Dissertation Abstracts International* 22 (September 1961): 852.

*Kirby, John B. "The New Deal Era and Blacks: A Study of Black and White Race Thought, 1933-1945." Ph.D. dissertation, University of Illinois, 1971.

Martin, Charles H. "Negro Leaders, The Republican Party and the Election of 1932." *Phylon* 32 (Spring 1971): 85-93.

*McCoy, Donald R. and Ruetten, Richard T. "The Civil Rights Movement: 1940-1954." *Mid-West Quarterly* 11 (October 1969): 11-34.

Meier, August and Rudwick, Elliott. "How CORE Began." *Social Science Quarterly* 49 (March 1969): 789-99.

———. "Negro Protest at the Chicago World's Fair, 1933-1934." *Illinois State Historical Society Journal* 59 (Summer 1966): 161-71.

Rudwick, Elliott M. "Oscar DePriest and the Jim Crow Restaurant in the U.S. House of Representatives." *Journal of Negro Education* 35 (Winter 1966): 77-82.

*Salmond, John A. "The Civilian Conservation Corps and the Negro." *Journal of American History* 52 (June 1965): 75-88.

*Sitkoff, Harvard, "The Detroit Race Riot of 1943." *Michigan Historical* 53 (Fall 1969): 183-201.

Ware, Gilbert. "Lobbying as a Means of Protest: The NAACP as an Agent of Equality." *Journal of Negro Education* 33 (Spring 1964): 103-10.

Weisbord, Robert and Stein, Arthur. "Negro Perceptions of Jews between the World Wars." *Judaism* 43 (Fall 1969): 428-47.

*Weiss, Nancy. "Not Alms but Opportunity: A History of the National Urban League, 1910-1940." Ph.D. dissertation, Harvard University, 1970.

Wittner, Lawrence S. "The National Negro Congress: A Reassessment." *American Quarterly* 22 (Winter 1970): 883-901.

*Wolters, Raymond R. "Section 7a and the Black Worker." *Labor Historical* 10 (Summer 1969): 459-474.

*———. "The Negro and the New Deal Economic Recovery Program." *Dissertation Abstracts International* 28 (January 1968): 2637A.

*Wynn, Neil A. "The Impact of the Second World War on the American Negro." *Journal of Contemporary History* 6, no. 2 (1971): 42-53.

*Zangrando, Robert L. "Efforts of the National Association for the Advancement of Colored People to Secure Passage of a Federal Anti-Lynching Law, 1920-1940." *Dissertation Abstracts International* 24 (April 1964): 41-69.

*———. "The NAACP and a Federal Anti-Lynching Bill, 1934-1940." *Journal of Negro History* 50 (April 1965): 106-17.

*———. "The Organized Negro: The National Association for the Advancement of Colored People and Civil Rights." In James C. Curtis and Lewis L. Gould, eds. *The Black Experience in America,* pp. 145-71. Austin: University of Texas Press, 1970.

*Copies in Franklin D. Roosevelt Library

The National Historical Publications and Records Commission's Committee on the Publication of Papers Relating to Blacks

EDGAR A. TOPPIN

The paper is concerned with the accomplishments and functions of the Special Advisory Committee to the National Historical Publications and Records Commission (NHPRC), a committee that solicits the publication of papers by prominent blacks.

The United States was relatively late in setting up an archives. Members of the American Historical Association (AHA), such as Franklin Jamison, had supported this idea as early as 1888. Nothing was done until the Roosevelt administration, when an advisory committee was set up to make suggestions as to what holdings might be included in such an archives. Construction of the building began in 1931 and was almost completed when Congress finally passed the legislation in 1934 to establish an organization called the National Archives.

That act also provided for a commission (NHPRC) that was charged with the responsibility of searching out and encouraging the publication of papers of individuals and institutions significant in the history of America. The documentary records of the ratification of the Constitution of the United States were the first set of papers to be encouraged by the NHPRC. The commission, which was organized in 1934, was hampered somewhat

George Washington Carver (RG 200, Gift Collection, no. 200(S)-HNP-13)

in its operation in that it did not have a full staff. It simply operated through National Archives staff members. The commission could not make final decisions on its own. Instead it merely made recommendations that had to be approved by Congress, and Congress, of course, selected the documents on the ratification of the Constitution as the first project.

In 1950 this method of selection of documents was changed, due to the passage of the Federal Records Act of that year, which gave the NHPRC the power to determine what projects would be encouraged, instituted, and funded. At that time, the commission appointed a staff and was able to function much more as an organization, but it still did not have the funds to institute projects. Consequently, it merely encouraged foundations, schools, institutions, and other organized groups to publish various collections of papers. A number of projects on prominent Americans such as Jefferson, Franklin, Madison, and others were eventually instituted under the aegis of this newly constituted commission.

The commission reported to the president because it was a presidential advisory commission. It reported to the president through the administrator of the General Services Administration concerning projects that needed to be undertaken. In the 1954 report, the names of several hundred persons, as well as some institutions, were suggested as topics. Singled out for special mention were 112 suggestions, but among that 112 Booker T. Washington was the only black listed. Among the individuals whose papers were recommended without any detailed description were two other blacks: George Washington Carver, and Robert R. Moton.

Subsequently, the NHPRC was given greater authority, beginning with recommendations made in 1961 which permitted it to fund projects. Although the initial authorization was approximately five hundred thousand dollars annually, the commission was appropriated only three hundred thousand dollars. Today the authorization is approximately two million dollars, although the appropriation lags far behind, at the half million dollar level.

The wider authority gained by the NHPRC during the 1960s also permitted the establishment of a special advisory committee, which included persons on the commission and outside individuals and scholars, to recommend for publication the papers of various blacks. The Committee on the Publication of Papers of Women was also established. Among the women whose papers this committee recommended be published were Mary McLeod Bethune and Mary Church Terrell.

The NHPRC is a highly structured organization. The chairperson is the archivist of the United States. There is one representative from the House and one from the Senate, the former appointed by the Speaker of the House, the latter by the president of the Senate. There is a representative from the Supreme Court. There are representatives from the Defense Department and State Department, since these agencies are very much involved with documents likely to have great historical import and the publication of such

Booker T. Washington (RG 200, Gift
Collection, no. 200(S)-HNP-44B)

documents. There are two presidential appointees selected from among
outstanding scientists, including social scientists. And there are representatives from the AHA.

In 1972 an amendment to the 1934 act permitted the Organization of
American Historians to appoint two members to the NHPRC. At that time,
I was appointed to the commission and became the first black to serve on
the commission in all the years of its existence.

The NHPRC has always been concerned about publishing the papers of
prominent blacks. As early as the 1954 report, the collections of three
blacks—Washington, Carver, and Moton—were suggested for publication. It is interesting to note that the three individuals singled out at that
time were all affiliated with Tuskegee Institute and all were more on the
moderate, if not conservative, side of the spectrum. Although whenever I
mention conservative in reference to blacks, I am reminded of the French
nobleman who scoffed and asked, when told that there was such a thing as a
black conservative, "Conservative? What do they have to conserve?"

In 1969 two members of the commission, Arthur Link, the noted
historian at Princeton and the editor of the Woodrow Wilson Papers, and
Whitefield Bell, the president of the American Philosophical Society, were
assigned to solicit the recommendations of scholars concerning the publication of papers by blacks. They sent out a number of letters to the scholars,
but did not get a very good response. They did learn several things: One,
that everyone seemed to agree that the two persons whose papers deserved

Frederick Douglass (RG 200, Gift Collection, no. 200(S)-FL-22)

to be published were those of Booker T. Washington and Frederick Douglass, with W.E.B. Du Bois rating third on the list. With regard to institutions, the scholars felt that the papers of the NAACP and the National Urban League should be published.

The Special Advisory Committee to the NHPRC is comprised of five other individuals: John Chavis at Tuskegee Institute; Louis Harlan at the University of Maryland and editor of the Booker T. Washington Papers; Michael R. Winston, director of the Moorland-Spingarn Research Center at Howard University; Otey Scruggs at Syracuse University; and Arthur Strickland at the University of Missouri at Columbia.

At its first meeting, the Special Advisory Committee began to explore the whole realm of problems connected with selecting for publication papers of blacks. The committee attempted to decide whether or not to restrict the work to the period that the National Archives usually recommends, i.e., papers of individuals who have been dead for at least twenty-five years.

The committee also discussed restricting the publication to blacks or to persons such as a John Brown or an Oliver Otis Howe, whose lives and work had an impact on the status of blacks in America. Other questions regarding selection criteria included (1) focusing on individuals or organizations; (2) the relevance of a collection's location or accessibility; and (3) the degree to which papers should be sufficiently rich in quantity and quality to merit consideration.

At present the committee is examining a group of papers that we simply agreed at the outset deserved immediate attention. The group includes the papers of the NAACP; the National Urban League; the National Association of Colored Women; the National Negro Business League; Sen. Blanche K. Bruce; George Washington Carver; Paul Cuffy; Marcus Garvey; the Grimké family; James Weldon Johnson; P.B.S. Pinchback; the Terrell family, including Mary Church Terrell and her husband Judge Robert H. Terrell; and Carter G. Woodson. These papers are tentative selections whose merit the committee will examine in much greater detail.

One of the problems identified with the preservation of the papers is that of accessioning. The University of Massachusetts at Amherst has purchased the papers of W.E.B. Du Bois from Herbert Aptheker. The purchase price of $150,000, which will no doubt be well publicized throughout the country, will simply compound the problem of convincing blacks to donate collections. Many people, who perhaps previously donated such papers for historical scholarship, will now no doubt agree that if Du Bois rated $150,000, their fathers or grandfathers undoubtedly would rate at least $149,999. Therefore, we foresee a great deal of competition and pressures in that sense.

A second problem is that of funding. The NHPRC has only a half million dollars, and this obviously will not pay for the preservation of a large

W. E. B. Du Bois (RG 200, Gift Collection no. 200(S)-HNP-16)

number of papers, nor can we count on other foundations and universities for financial assistance.

Aside from the NHPRC, there are other institutions that are sponsoring the preservation of valuable collections. The University of Maryland is

Mary Church Terrell (RG 200, Gift Collection, no 200(S)-HNP-40)

assisting with the editing of the Booker T. Washington Papers. Currently, seven volumes have been published. Louis Harlan is editor and Raymond W. Smock is coeditor of this series. John Blassingame is editing the Frederick Douglass Papers, which are being funded by Yale University. One volume of this series has been published. And the John Hope Franklin Papers have been microfilmed and will soon be ready for circulation. Alton Hornsby of Morehouse College is editor of these papers.

The NHPRC solicits the support of scholars in locating collections, in helping to refine selection criteria, and in bringing to the committee's attention the papers of deserving blacks and institutions that, once published, will greatly illuminate the history of blacks in America.

V

Afro-American Social History Based on Federal Archives: The Family

The Other Side of Slavery

ANDREW BILLINGSLEY
MARILYN CYNTHIA GREENE

In American scholarship few events have been subjected to the kind of extensive analysis as has the institution called slavery, its origins, its developments, its destruction, and its consequences. Yet, despite such massive scholarly inquiry, and because scholarship is generally a reflection of the values, interests, and preoccupations of the larger society of which it is a part, the studies of American slavery are not yet exhaustive. There is more to be learned about this series of events that will add to the storehouse of world knowledge and perhaps world civilization.

This paper examines some of the aspects of slavery that have not been as fully examined as others. For example, a great deal of the research on slavery is done from the standpoint and, indeed, from the vantage point of the perpetrators of the system. Our research is focused on the experiences of the victims of the system. Most of the information and theories about slavery are based on studies of larger plantations. In ''The Other Side of Slavery,'' we give major attention to the lives of slaves on smaller farms and on nonfarm units where the majority of Africans lived. Some of the literature of slavery is focused on large-scale political, legal, military, economic, and social forces surrounding that institution, and much of the literature ignores the patterns of relationships among the Africans and the more intimate aspects of these relationships. Most studies either assume or assert the nonexistence of organized family life among the slaves.

This paper focuses on the family life of slaves, searching for the existence, manifestations, patterning, and the consequences of organized forms of family life among the slaves. Our aim is to add to the body of knowledge about the life of the African people during this particular period in our history and in the history of the Republic.

The National Archives has been a primary source of data, as well as the Library of Congress, the state archives of Maryland and Virginia, the Moorland collection at Howard University, and the special collections housed in the Schomburg Collection in New York, and at Fisk, Atlanta, and Dillard universities. Much of the research for this paper grew out of the work reported in *Black Families in White America*.[1]

This study of family life among Africans during and immediately after slavery may be termed sociological in the sense that the focus of our search is on patterns of relationships—intimate relationships among the slaves—which may be conceived as familial, and to examine both the causes and the consequences of these patterns of behavior, if they exist. Because sociologists have been trained so little in history, this study poses for us a number of very challenging problems, and offers very exciting learning experiences.

"Did family life exist among the Africans during slavery?" It is not an idle nor a simple question. Insofar as that question has been addressed at all by American scholars, the predominant answer would be, "No." There are exceptions, of course, and among a new stream of scholarship—including the works of John Blassingame, Benjamin Quarles, Lawrence Reddick, George Warwick, and Herbert Gutman—the answer is more affirmative. Among still other scholars the question is not yet considered a legitimate one.

This debate is similar to that which surrounded the investigation of Afro-American spirituals prior to studies such as John Lovell's definitive work, *Black Song: The Forge and the Flame*. Professor Lovell titled the first chapter of this work, "Is There an Afro-American Spiritual?" He observed:

> To open an investigation by asking if the subject really exists would normally be most peculiar. But not so if one had just finished reading three thousand plus references on the so-called Negro spiritual and its background.

He continued:

> From a 360-degree perspective of mountains of comment, several things are clear: (1) Much has been written by self-styled interpreters who were only partially supplied with reliable evidence. (2) From any consistent viewpoint the basic *African* and *American* elements have been confused

and misread. (3) Vested interests on all sides, because of the high value placed on the songs, have fomented claims and conclusions that no reasonable analysis can justify.[2]

What John Lovell says about the study of the spiritual is also an accurate description of the state of scholarship about Afro-American family life during the period of slavery. The question, then, of the existence of family life among the Africans during slavery, first answered by massive denials by American scholars, now partially opened by a new line of scholarly inquiry, is a legitimate one.

On the basis of our reading of the literature, we approach this question with what sociologists term the null hypothesis. First, we posit the view that black family life did not exist during slavery; that all vestiges of family life known in Africa were destroyed by slavery, and that the European-American patterns of family life practiced among the slavers and other white people were for slaves prohibited for a variety of commercial, political, and psychological reasons. The null hypothesis states that family life among the Africans trapped in the bondage of slavery did not exist. To determine whether a careful analysis of the data casts doubt on the null hypothesis, we examined a variety of sources.

In his work on the Negro in South Carolina during Reconstruction, Joel Williamson found that many black families had been established during slavery and continued to exist afterwards. He observed:

> Many Negroes emerged from slavery with orthodox family associations already well defined. For instance, in July, 1865, on a cotton plantation in Kershaw District, 121 of the 133 Negro residents belonged to 35 families. Of these families 32 were headed by a husband and wife, 2 by women alone, and 1 by a man alone. In ages, sizes and proportions between male and female these families were, apparently, entirely like those of the whites in the same time and place. On this particular plantation, all the younger children seem to have enjoyed secure family arrangements. Of the 43 children too young to be rated as quarter hands 33 had both mothers and fathers, 7 had only a mother, and 3 belonged to a wifeless father.[3]

For our purposes, the National Archives is rich in data important to establishing whether or not family life existed among black people during slavery. A major source that we have examined is the decennial population census schedules, from the very first U.S. census in 1790 through the census of 1880. These records are not complete or uniform, and certainly do not give uniform attention to the demographic characteristics of the black slaves or black freedpeople. But they are extensive, and a systematic analysis of these data sheds considerable light on the existence of black families during slavery, particularly among the 750,000 free blacks who in 1790 constituted roughly 8 percent of the total black population. By 1860 the black population had increased by 488,000, free blacks constituting 11 percent. This segment of the population should not be ignored when examining the existence of black families during slavery.

The Existence of Families Among
Free Blacks Prior to Emancipation

We know from the work of Letitia Woods Brown that during slavery the great majority of all free black people lived in Washington, D.C., Maryland, and Virginia, and most of the rest lived in New York, Pennsylvania, North and South Carolina. Brown also informs us that:

> While the majority of the persons of African descent in the Virginia-Maryland area were slaves, 20,909 were free. The 8,043 free Negroes in Maryland represented 13 percent of the 59,150 free Negroes in the United States, while the 12,866 in Virginia constituted 21 percent of the total. More than one-third of all free Negroes in the United States resided within the bounds of these two states. New York and Pennsylvania, the two Northern "free" states with the largest number of Negroes between them, stood next with less than 20 percent. While Virginia and Maryland were recognized then and in subsequent decades as "slave" states, free Negroes were a persistent part of the social structure of both provinces from the earliest days.[4]

Altogether there were roughly 753,000 persons of African descent in the continental United States at the time of the first census. Our own analysis suggests that family units were a significant aspect of the organized life among free blacks. In Baltimore County alone, the census takers counted thirty-six black families. Of these, twenty-four were headed by males and seven by females. The sex of the heads of five families is unknown because of the common practice among census takers of not listing first names for some of the black family heads. It may also be observed that the average number of persons in the thirty-six Baltimore County families was 3.5 and that both the male-headed and the female-headed families also had an average of 3.5 members. The prevailing practice in this census was to list only the given names of the family head. Only rarely were given names and surnames of other members of the family listed.

A brief inspection of the 1790 census data from Kent County, Maryland, reveals not only the names, sex of family heads, total family size, and color (labeled Negroes or Mulattoes), but also ownership of slaves by free black persons. Among free black families in Kent County in 1790, a total of twenty-four families had slaves. No doubt these were often relatives of the freedpeople. None of these family heads was a large plantation owner. The average number of slaves in each of these twenty-four families was 2.8; the largest number owned by any one family was eight. One family, headed by Lewis Gilbert, which included one other free person who was probably his wife, owned seven slaves. Another, headed by Samuel Golding, which included two other free persons, owned five slaves. The family headed by Amy Reece, which included two other free members, also owned five slaves. And the family headed by George Collins, which included one other free person, owned five slaves. The majority of these twenty-four families, however, owned one or two slaves at the most.

The spectre of black people, who may or may not have been enslaved themselves at some point, owning slaves after their own manumission—particularly the idea of blacks actively buying and selling their fellow Africans as chattel—raises the same kinds of questions raised by the participation in the slave trade by Africans in Africa, a number of whom sold their tribespeople into slavery. Ironically, some who participated in selling their fellow Africans played into the hands of the oppressors themselves. Robert R. Moton, who was for a time president of Tuskegee Institute and an in-law of the great Booker T. Washington, has told of the capture in Africa of one of his ancestors who had been party to selling other Africans into slavery:

> About the year of 1735, a fierce battle was waged between two strong tribes on the west coast of Africa. The chief of one of these tribes . . . overpowered his rival and slaughtered and captured a great number of his band. . . . The victorious chief delivered to his son about a dozen of this forlorn remnant, and he, with an escort, took them away to be sold into slavery. The young African pushed his way through the jungle with his bodyguard until he reached the coast. Arrived there, he sold his captives to the captain of an American slave ship and received his pay in trinkets of various kinds, common to the custom of the trade. Then he was asked to row out in a boat and inspect the wonderful ship. He went, and with the captain and the crew saw every part of the vessel. When it was all over they offered him food and he ate it heartily. After that he remembered no more till he woke to find himself in the hold of the ship chained to one of the miserable creatures whom he himself had so recently sold as a slave, and the vessel itself was far beyond the sight

of land. After many days the ship arrived at the shores of America; the
human cargo was brought to Richmond and this African slave merchant
was sold along with his captives at public auction in the slave markets
of the city. He was bought by a tobacco planter and carried to Amelia
County, Virginia, where he lived to be a very old man. This man was
my grandmother's great grandfather.[5]

In addition to the cruelty and duplicity it reveals, this excerpt establishes
the existence of familial ties among the slaves in this country, without
which Moton would not have been able to trace his ancestry through five
generations. It is similar to the story told so well by Alex Haley, who traced
his own family history back to the eighteenth century in a small village in
The Gambia, in West Africa.

There is still another aspect, however, to black persons owning slaves in
the United States at that time. Free blacks often were permitted to purchase
relatives, offspring, wives, or husbands. And they were not always in a
position to set them free at will. They were often only in a position to
provide better care and protection for them than would the ordinary slaveholders.

The analysis of the 1790 census data represents only the beginning of a
study of family life among slaves. All of the census data for selected states
from 1790 through 1880 should be subjected to computer analysis in order
to exploit these data fully for patterns of interrelationship among the
variables represented. At the same time qualitative data should be examined for clues to the causes and the consequences of the family patterns
described. Even so, such analysis may not be sufficient to overturn the null
hypothesis about the nonexistence of family life among the slaves. Our
work suggests, however, that such an analysis is sufficiently strong to call
into serious question the null hypothesis.

Even when the existence and patterning of family life among the freedpeople is established, the question will remain whether the family existed
among the slaves. We turn, then, to some observations from our analysis of
this aspect of the question.

The Existence of Families Among
Enslaved Africans in the United States

As in so many other aspects of the sociology of black people in America,
the most definitive work on the subject of family life among the enslaved

population has been done by E. Franklin Frazier, who was for the last twenty-five years of his life, professor and for a time, chairperson of the sociology department at Howard University. He was, of course, a world renowned scholar, and his work on the family, youth, the church, and the middle class have made inestimable contributions to knowledge about the life and conditions of Americans of African descent. Yet, some of the limitations of his work have become increasingly apparent to contemporary scholars.

Much of the contemporary scholarly assertions about the absence of family life among black people during slavery refers to the works of Frazier, principally his book *The Negro Family in the United States*.[6] Such references to Frazier's theories for the support of this null hypothesis reflect a superficial reading of this work and an almost total ignorance of Frazier's earlier more definitive studies as reflected in three of his works: "The Negro Slave Family,"[7] an article published in 1930; *The Free Negro Family*,[8] a monograph published in 1932; and *The Negro Family in Chicago*,[9] a book which also appeared in 1932. In each of these works the existence of family life among the enslaved population is generally recognized. In the opening of his study of Negro slave families, Frazier begins with a quote from another scholar: "But in spite of numerous exceptions, the marital and family rights of the slaves were perhaps generally recognized."[10] He also quotes from the work of Du Bois a more modest claim for the existence of slave families. After delineating the absence of legal sanctions and protections as the prevailing norm for family life among the enslaved population, Du Bois observes: "The point is that the recognition of the black family from 1619 to 1863 was purely a matter of individual judgment or caprice on the part of the master.[11]

In his own research, Frazier found that:

> The social life of the slaves, moreover, was safeguarded from much arbitrary outside interference by the sentiment on the part of masters against the molestation of their slaves, so long as their behavior was not a flagrant menace to social order.[12]

He also found in some slave families "a high degree of organization and a deep sense of family solidarity."[13] In his concluding statements, Frazier observed, "Where the plantation system was breaking down and Negro artisans achieved a semi-free status and acquired property, the slave family tended to become stabilized."[14] Thus, he points to the conditions under which family life was permitted to exist, the economic interests of the slaveholders being paramount, the social status of the slaves secondary.

Frazier, in a rather indirect manner, also calls attention to a basic cause of the existence of family life that emanated from among the African people themselves. After referring to the economic preconditions for the existence of family stability, he observed:

> In such cases the slave family was held together by more than the affectional bonds that developed naturally among its members through the association in the same household and the affection of parents for their offspring.[15]

Our own study may be viewed as a continuation of the pioneering work on family life during slavery conducted by Frazier. An analysis of the documents in the National Archives as well as a systematic analysis of autobiographies, slave narratives, and other writings of the slaves and ex-slaves, as well as careful reading of contemporary historians who are providing fresh sources of data and interpretations of that period in the life of black people should be expanded.

In this paper we refer principally to two sources of data made available to us in the National Archives, which bear on the existence of relatively stable forms of family life among the enslaved people of African descent. The regular decennial censuses conducted between 1790 and 1860 did not identify the enslaved people by name. Slaves were listed and enumerated as property, but the Freedmen's Bureau did conduct a special census after the end of the Civil War which did enumerate ex-slaves by name. In addition, we have examined the records of special marriage registries established by the bureau which allowed former slaves who had been married in informal ceremonies to have their marriages legalized and registered. These registries were established in a dozen locations throughout the former slaveholding region of the country. In this paper we present a preliminary analysis of data collected in Washington, D.C., in 1867 and in Vicksburg, Mississippi, between 1864 and 1866. These data speak directly to the existence of families among the enslaved people, which often endured many years during the period of slavery.

Between November 1866 and July 1867, 843 couples who had been married and lived together during slavery came to have their marriages legalized and registered in the District of Columbia. Among these were

Freedmen's Bureau marriage register. (RG 105, Bureau of Refugees, Freedmen, and Abandoned Lands)

Bureau Refugees, Freedmen, and Abandoned Lands.

Headquarters Ass't Commissioner, District Columbia,

Washington, July 5th, 1867.

Bvt. Lt. Col. H. H. Rogers.
          A.A.A. General.
                    Colonel:
                              I have the honor to
report that the number of Certificates of Legal Marriage
granted during the month of June, by Rev. W. V. Wright,
Assistant Superintendent of Marriages, is one hundred and
ninety-four (194). The children of these parties number
five hundred and thirty eight (538). One hundred and
fourteen (114) of these Couples are from Virginia, seventy-
one (71) from Maryland, five (5) from the District of Columbia,
two (2) from Georgia, one (1) from Alabama and one (1)
from North Carolina.
                    Mr. Wright has found forty-three (43) Couples
living together illegally as husband and wife, ~~and these~~

having, twenty-four children.   The names of persons
living thus illigally together at Campbell Hospital, are

Danl. Johnson and Maria Saxon

Joseph Mitchell .   Elizabeth Smoot

William Scott .   Suey Fox.

James Nelson   „   Agnes Buckner

John Butler   „   Jane Butler

At Wisewell Barracks

James Harris and Amanda Coleman.

Churchhill Wethers „   Minnie Wethers.

Mr. Wright thinks it will take about Two (2)
months longer to complete the work.

Date	Minister	Names of Husband and Wife		Former Residence	When Married
Nov. 1866	R. H. Robinson	Humphrey Ware	Catherine Stone	Charles Co. Md.	1862
"	"	"	Charles Duvall	Mary J. Abram	Colbert Co. "	1862
"	"	"	William Duvall	Margret Johnson	Anne Arundell Co.	1855
"	"	"	Dobson Ware	Jane Miles	Charles Co. "	1855
"	"	"	Charles Thomas	Ellen Furguson	Washington. D.C.	1832
"	"	"	James Williams	Nelly Brooks	Prince George Co. Md.	1846
"	"	"	Clement Smith	Ann C. Tinekum	Charles Co. "	1860
"	"	"	Thos. Blackburn	Harriet Masterson	Fairfax Co. Va.	1852
"	"	"	William Jackson	Sarah Johnson	Charles Co. Md.	1855
"	"	"	Walter Young	Rosa Johnson	" " "	1862
"	"	"	George Strother	Mary Gray	Not Stated	1831
"	"	"	Jeremiah Grandison	Harriet Holland	Montgomery Co. Md.	1862
"	"	"	Charles West	Henrietta Chase	Not Stated	1836
"	"	"	George Shelton	Susan Jasper	Alexandria Va.	1860
"	"	"	Samuel Barnard	Rebecca Berry	Prince George Co. Md.	1836
"	"	"	Richard Dalany	Alla Brownin	" " "	1836
"	"	"	Andrew Smith	Matel da Miles	" " "	1826
"	"	"	Samuel Jackson	Jane Miller	Shreveport. La.	1856
"	"	"	Andrew Lingum	Sarah Boston	Anne Arundell Co. Md.	1836
"	"	"	Mottro Johnson	Rachael Colbert	Prince George Co. Md.	1846
"	"	"	Lewis Ridgley	Mary Watters	" " "	1855
"	"	"	Alex. Stewart	Mary Henson	" " "	1862
"	"	"	William Davis	Lettie Foster	" " "	1863
"	"	"	Osborn Jackson	Mary Vigal	Georgetown. D.C.	1846
"	"	"	Wm Pratt.	Martha Lovers	Anna Arundell Co. Md.	1858
"	"	"	Wm Henson	Eliza Stewart	Prince George Co. "	1856
"	"	"	Nathaniel Colbert	Amelia Henson	" " "	1844
"	"	"	Thomas Johnson	Elizabeth Mockley	" " "	1860
"	"	"	Mott Bell	Jane Smith	" " "	1836
"	"	"	Wm H. Brown	Mary E. Harris	Washington. D.C.	1845
"	"	"	Spencer Briscoe	Maria Simms	Prince George Co. Md.	1846
"	"	"	Sand. Ferguson	Harriett Tilgman	" " "	1857
"	"	"	Moses Hall	Mary Hodge	Anne Arundell Co. "	1860
"	"	"	Washington Hutton	Harriett Bacon	" " "	1841
"	"	"	Henry Wiggs	Eliza Wyson	Prince George Co. Md.	1840
"	"	"	Albert Jackson	Henrietta Wood	Loudon Co. Va.	1845

Charles West and Henrietta Chase, both ex-slaves, who in November 1866 had their marriage registered by Rev. R.H. Robinson. They had been given permission to marry in 1836 but had not had a ceremony. When they registered in November 1866, they had nine children and had lived together for nearly thirty years. During the same month in 1866, Isaac Diggs and Letty Smith, both ex-slaves, had their marriage registered by Rev. J.A. Jones. They had been married for forty years, first joined together by Rev. Breckinbridge in Prince Georges County, Maryland, in 1826 by permission of their owner. At the time they registered they also had nine children. In May of 1867 George Washington and Mary Shanklin had their marriage registered by M.V. Wright. They had been married in 1847 in King George County, Virginia, in a ceremony conducted by Moses Myers. They were the parents of nine children.

Of the 843 couples, ten had been married to each other for over forty years, and 47 had been married for over twenty years, or since before 1845. Over 140 couples married originally in 1860 and 1861, the years of secession and the outbreak of the Civil War. Only 5 had married for the first time at the end of, or after, the war.

Despite the fact that these couples had been married for a very long time, the wives maintained separate surnames. This was a very common practice. Among the 843 couples who had their marriages registered in the District of Columbia, only 21 of them had adopted the same or common surname. Altogether 97 of these couples had originally been married by a minister, roughly 284 had been married in a ceremony conducted by their owner or other individuals, and 462 others married either without ceremony or the name of the officiator was not recorded.

Most of the couples that had their marriage registered in Washington, D.C., were originally married in Maryland or Virginia. However, there were a few exceptions. (Table 1 shows the state of the former residence of each of these couples without respect to the year in which they got married.)

The selected examples are of families with large numbers of children. Among the families who were known to have children, the average number was 3.4. Not all families were large. Altogether 135 families had only one child, 168 had two, 142 had three, and 76 had four children.

The major finding of the previously cited data from a Washington, D.C., registry is that family life did indeed exist among a number of enslaved people in Maryland and Virginia for many years before the end of the Civil War.

Table 1

STATE OF ORIGIN OF COUPLES REGISTERING MARRIAGE IN THE DISTRICT OF COLUMBIA, NOVEMBER 1866 THROUGH JULY 1867

State of Origin	Number of Families
Maryland	281
Virginia	499
Washington, D.C.	39
North Carolina	2
Louisiana	3
Georgia	4
Alabama	1
West Indies	1
Not stated	5
Unknown	8
Total	843

Source: District of Columbia Marriage Record, 1866 and 1867, Record Group 105, NA.

In Vicksburg, Mississippi, between 1864 and 1866 altogether 4,638 couples who had been married during slavery had their marriages registered. In the vast majority of these families, almost 75 percent of the husbands were older than the wives. In less than 20 percent of these families were the wives older. (Table 2 shows the comparative age breakdown.)

The number of children each of these couples had varied from zero to a dozen or more. Altogether 41 percent of them had one child, and 73 percent had two to four children.

Table 2

COMPARATIVE AGE OF MARRIED COUPLE

	Number	Percentage
Men older	3,454	74.4
Women older	853	17.6
Couple same age	291	6.2
Data not available	40	1.8
Total	4,638	100.0

Source: Marriage Records, Assistant Commissioner, Vicksburg, Mississippi, 1863-1866, RG 105, NA.

Many partners in the marriages registered after the Civil War had had prior marriages. Tables 3 and 4 contain data on those unions and their offspring.

Table 3

MEN WITH PREVIOUS SPOUSE

	Number	Percentage
No previous spouse	2,586	55.8
Previous spouse	1,893	40.8
Indicated having children, previous, but gave no information on previous spouse	159	3.4
Total	4,638	100.0
Number of years with previous spouse		
1 or less	272	13.3
2-4	599	29.2
5-10	635	31.0
11 and over	387	18.8
Data not available	159	7.7
Total	2,052	100.0
Number of children by previous marriage		
None	879	42.8
1	371	18.1
2-4	552	26.9
5-10	215	10.5
11 or more	36	1.7
Total	2,053	100.0

Source: Marriage Records, Assistant Commissioner, Vicksburg, Mississippi, 1863-1866, RG 105, NA.

There were a variety of reasons that the prior marriages were dissolved. Principally, they were dissolved by the owner by force, sometimes by simple insistence and beatings, and sometimes by the sale of a partner in a marriage. Next in order of frequency was death of the spouse. (Table 5 shows a breakdown of the reasons for separation from their previous spouses.)

Table 4

WOMEN WITH PREVIOUS SPOUSE

	Number	Percentage
No previous spouse	2,409	51.9
Previous spouse	2,038	43.9
Indicated having children, previous, but gave no information on previous spouse	191	4.2
Total	4,638	100.0
Number of years with previous spouse		
1 or less	333	14.9
2-4	709	31.8
5-10	703	31.6
11 and over	293	13.1
Data not available	191	8.6
Total	2,234	100.0
Number of children by previous marriage		
None	968	44.0
1	434	19.7
2-4	607	27.6
5-10	192	8.7
Total	2,201	100.0

Source: Marriage Records, Assistant Commissioner, Vicksburg, Mississippi, 1863-1866, RG 105, NA.

Table 5

REASONS FOR SEPARATION FROM PREVIOUS SPOUSES

	Male	Percentage	Female	Percentage
Death	775	41.6	1,103	55.8
Force	872	46.9	688	34.8
Desertion	95	5.1	90	4.5
Consent	97	5.2	81	4.1
Other	24	1.2	14	.8
Total	1,863	100.0	1,976	100.0

Source: Marriage Records, Assistant Commissioner, Vicksburg, Mississippi, 1863-1866, RG 105, NA.

The previously analyzed data from both the Washington, D.C. registry and the Vicksburg, Mississippi, registry show that the existence of family life among black people during slavery was not confined to free black families or to any one section of the country. These data are not sufficient to show a complete picture. They are only a portion of our continuing analysis. They do allow us to proceed with an examination of the general hypothesis about the nonexistence of black family life during slavery with confidence that it may eventually be overturned. In addition to continuing this analysis, therefore, we will also turn our attention to some of the qualitative aspects of black family life during this period as our study proceeds, with the aim of adding to the storehouse of knowledge about the sources of survival and achievement among this great people during a most oppressive phase of existence in this country.

NOTES

1. Andrew Billingsley, *Black Families in White America* (Englewood Cliffs, N.J.: Prentice-Hall, 1968), p. 15.
2. John Lovell, Jr., *Black Song: The Forge and the Flame* (New York: Macmillan Company, 1972), p. 3.
3. Joel Williamson, *After Slavery: The Negro in South Carolina during Reconstruction* (Chapel Hill: The University of North Carolina Press, 1965), p. 306.
4. Letitia Woods Brown, *Free Negroes in the District of Columbia, 1790-1846* (New York: Oxford University Press, 1972), p. 17.
5. Robert R. Moton, *Finding a Way Out* (Wilmington, N.C.: Consortium Press, 1969), p. 37.
6. E. Franklin Frazier, *The Negro Family in the United States* (Chicago: University of Chicago Press, 1939), p. 15.
7. Idem, "The Negro Slave Family," *Journal of Negro History* 15 (April 1930): 198.
8. Idem, *The Free Negro Family* (Nashville: Fisk University Press, 1932), p. 16.
9. Idem, *The Negro Family in Chicago* (Chicago: University of Chicago Press, 1932), p. 17.
10. Ibid., p. 198.
11. Ibid.
12. Ibid., p. 206.
13. Ibid., p. 233.
14. Ibid., p. 259.
15. Frazier, *The Free Negro Family*, p. 16.

Familial Values
of Freedmen and Women

HERBERT G. GUTMAN

The familial and sexual values of freedmen and women have been gravely and profoundly misunderstood and misinterpreted by most historians and sociologists almost since these two disciplines took shape as professional work. This confusion continues to rest on many severe misconceptions.* Some, but not all, are rooted in racial beliefs. Others have their origin in a woefully inadequate methodology that has made a jumble of the social history of the American lower classes. A methodology that allows us to comprehend everyday historical beliefs and behavior of ordinary men and women, blacks among them, is still to be worked out by American social historians.

This paper suffers from several disadvantages. First, what has been written about the black family in the past is of little use, and the methodology available is at best yet primitive for rewriting it. Second, the primary sources available for research are massive in quantity. That is to say, there is no end to the materials available to those who are concerned with reconstructing the familial and sexual as well as the general beliefs and behavior of the emancipated population.

Still another difficulty in presenting so brief a paper is that there is nearly no limit to what these materials can reveal about the freed blacks, and most significantly, about the enslaved themselves. For researchers who want to study the records of those Afro-Americans who lived in slavery between

*This essay was delivered as a talk prior to the publication of *The Black Family in Slavery and Freedom, 1750-1925* (1976). The author had not yet started to reexamine the slave family and kin group.

1830 and 1860, and knew emancipation either as adult men and women or as young children, the richest sources are those found in the records of the federal army and of the Freedmen's Bureau.

Materials in the army and bureau records have disadvantages that deserve special attention. But compared to other available sources, these materials are relatively free of biases and, as others have pointed out, record regularly the direct testimony from blacks themselves, including large numbers of former slave field hands. Such testimony is of great value when measured against the other available major sources such as the records kept by southern whites and the observations about the emancipated blacks reported by northern missionaries, army officers, and school-teachers.

In dealing with the records kept by southern whites (so far as the family is concerned), it is sufficient to mention that southern white newspapers, during Reconstruction and for decades thereafter, rarely, if ever, described a married southern black woman as "Mrs." And what is there to say of the northern missionary men and women who found evidence of "savagery" among the emancipated blacks because few men and women wore under-clothes. The army and bureau records, then, are a potentially massive correction to the biases built into those records that have traditionally been used to examine the moral, social, familial, and sexual values of black men and women before and just after emancipation.

One may ask, "How can army and bureau records reveal so much, if anything, about the enslaved?" In examining these records, a methodological distinction needs to be made and emphasized. Cultural anthropologists make a critical, analytic distinction between culture and society. Professor Sidney Mintz finds in culture "a kind of resource" and in society "a kind of arena." "The distinction," he writes, "being between sets of historically available alternatives or forms on the one hand and circumstances or society within which these forms may be employed on the other."

Emancipation altered the societal circumstances in which southern blacks, former slaves, lived. But emancipation did not radically transform the culture of the enslaved. It is therefore possible to examine the behavior of the recently emancipated and learn about the beliefs and values they held during enslavement. From this evidence we can also learn much about the adaptive capacities of enslaved Afro-Americans.

One kind of archival record dealing with familial and moral beliefs among the freedmen and women is examined briefly in this paper. Such evidence reveals many of the gross inadequacies of the currently fashionable theories meant to explain the behavior of slaves and the behavior and beliefs of freed southern blacks. It deals with the freedmen's powerful exercise of their protective role as fathers and husbands. The evidence cited in this discussion was drawn entirely from materials in the bureau records, and that material has been made available to me and to many others by the National Archives staff. I acknowledge my debt and that of many other persons to that staff for making available to social historians so much rich new material.

The proponents of one popular model of male slave behavior contend that although slaves had families, male members could not play effective roles as fathers or husbands. This paper contains data that reveal parental and husbandly authority among former slave field hands in the months following emancipation.

Evidence describing how former slaves, nearly all field hands, sought protection for their recently freed families is found in the bureau complaint registers and the military and bureau court records, and in the general and military records for the year and a half or two years following the war. Let me illustrate the types of materials one finds. These differ from Leon Litwack's evidence of collective complaints. They are individual complaints by males. An Alabama black, Isaac Calley, for example, charged in October 1865 that J.B. Connaly, for whom he and his wife worked, had denied them wages. Then pregnant, the black's wife had labored as a house servant until Connaly told her to quit the place. She wanted to leave, but the white refused to pay her. Isaac Calley went to the bureau to file a complaint.

That same year, blacks in large numbers over the entire South filed similar complaints. The former Barnwell County, South Carolina, field hand, Handy Parker, complained that his wife and two sons had been hidden from Sherman's army by their owner and that Parker had left with the occupying army. Parker's wife and sons later planted a crop for the former white owner, and after it matured, they were, as the complaint read, "brutally whipped and ordered off from the place." Parker's wife reported the assaults to an army officer (who cautioned the former white owner) but on her return she was whipped again. Handy Parker asked the federal army for authority to go to his former owner, take his family, and secure, as he put it, a proper portion of "what his family had raised."

The Pineville, South Carolina, black, Johnson Ravenell, had a different problem. He and other blacks had planted a crop for their former owner, James Gegman, but quit because Gegman had whipped the male Daniel and Ravenell's sister-in-law "upon her naked body." Ravenell also wanted help in restoring property that Gegman withheld from him, and complained that he had been unable to get his wife away from Gegman's place.

Jacob Sadler went before the Barnwell Bureau to protest the abuse of his son Samuel Eubanks. Whites had broken into his son's house and tied and chained the young man to a tree. Sadler quit the place to report their action to the army. He said that his son had been sick at the time and had as a witness a local white named Jack MacDonald who swore that Samuel had been chained to the tree for forty-eight hours.

Husbands and fathers in other parts of the South made similar complaints. George Washington, for example, contracted in 1866 with the Virginia white, R.H. Horner, to be paid $140 and supplied with food and medical care for the year. Later that year, Washington said the white drew a pistol on his wife because of something she had said ''in reference to her not having time to keep the white children's clothing clean.'' After that the family subsisted, as he put it, almost entirely on apples. And then Horner paid Washington $75. Washington pressed for full payment before the Alexandria, Virginia, Freedmen's Bureau.

Complaints filed in central Tennessee by Murfreesburo blacks revealed the range of concerns among black males for their families. All of these complaints were filed between July and December 1865 and deserve special notice in examining the roles played by free black males. Martin McCullough, a black, charged that James McCullough, a white, had killed his mother and father earlier that year because they no longer wished to work for him. In another incident, Jack Turner said that when his wife had sought payment for services from a white, she had been beaten. The military authorities ordered that she be paid $15.

Anthony (last name not available) charged that William Murray ''severely beat my wife and daughter with a stick because we were singing a Union song.'' Shortly after being ordered before the bureau, Murray died of apoplexy. Another complaint concerned William Stover who said that in the presence of ten whites and one black a former owner had ''put two pistol shots through the right arm of his younger sister.''

On July 28, 1865, a black named Ben (last name not available) pressed charges against a former owner, Beverley Randolph. ''Ben pressed charges. Ben says that on the 29th of June Randolph beat my wife with his fists, then caught her by the chin, threw back her head, pulled out his knife, and swore that he would cut her throat. The woman was large with a child at the time.'' The bureau made Randolph pay a $55 fine.

Sept 14th   Tina (Col'd) vs Ubidow Brothers
"   Tina Says I live with Ubidow Brothers on
"   Fall Creek 13 miles — Mr May the overseer
"   tied me up because I would not consent to
"   him & tied my Clothes around my neck.
"   & beat me very badly then drove me off
"   without pay or a morsel to eat —
   (Said girl 19 years old was whelted all over
      Shamefully)
   Mrs Brothers & Albert Jones Administrator came
   on order & stated they knew nothing of the
   beating untill the next day   May ran off
   to Georgia
11th "   Unity & Minerva vs D Beasely
"   Unity is 70 years of age & Suckled Beasely
"   Minerva is 45 & with her Beasely has cohabited
"   nightly for 17 Years (they have laid in the same
"   bed that time at nights)   At the fight at Stone River
"   Beasely left his home (a poor one) & told the
"   2 Cold Women the Black hearted Yankees were
"   Coming they might stay & have everything he
   left — he was going to his Children — he left

*A Freedmen's Bureau report on outrages, riots, and other crimes committed
in the state of Tennessee.* (RG 105, Bureau of Refugees, Freedmen, and
Abandoned Lands)

" and after an absence of a year he returns
" & Drives us into the Street
. The Cohabitation he did not deny & drove
" the old woman off because she could not work
" & Minerva because she would not submit
" to his lust — Ordered him to permit them
to stay rent free & pay 9 Dollars rent paid
else where while driven off & threatened with
Imprisonment if he ever urged his baseness
an either -

2nd   Israel Huntsman from Ohio & Agent
" for a Carriage factory in Crawford County Ohio
" goes through the Country as a US Agent
" Collecting taxes from the Colored Race to
" purchase them homes (with a Six Shooter)
"   I arrested him & proved abtaining money
under false pretenses Sent to prison untill
he paid a fine of fifty dollars — he remained
3 Weeks paid his fine obtain by letter from
his home & I paid him 5 Dolls to send him home
25 to the negroes he had Cheated & 15 to 3 families
to help them to go to Georgia & 5 for Stationery

Dec.r 10th Sundry Laborers Vs Peter Goodin
" Said Laborers Say   they worked all the year
" for P.r Goodin & last week he called in the due bills
" he gave us & paid us 20 per cent & promised to met
" us all at the Bureau to pay the ballance—he left on
" the Cars yesterday & has Cheated us all (gone to Napoleon
" Arkansas)

Nov 27.th   Tabby Wheatly, Vs Andrew B Payne
" Tabby Says on Monday 27 Inst Payne took my
" daughter & beat her badly—She came to my Cabin
" & Payne & Miles Ferguson with him they wanted to
" beat the girl more I would not let them Payne then
" Jumped on me & Ferguson Struck me a Dozen times
" with a Stick Payne took the girl down the back
" of the Yard & Pulled her Clothes over her head & beat her
" holding his head between his knees — I heard the cries
" of the girl & ran down he then let go the Girl & began
" to beat me again   By order Payne appeared &
       confessed to the beating but denied that he
       sanctioned Fergusons acts
       Fined 25 Dolls. Paid Plaintiff
          (This is Payne's 2nd Outrage)

Five weeks later, Bee Whitney made a similar accusation against his former white owner and then employer, Rucker. The bureau sent a military guard to arrest Rucker. The white confessed, paid $50, and gave the dispossessed couple $400 in back wages.

Husbands and fathers in and near Grenada, Mississippi, most of whom were former field hands, filed complaints similar to those made by North Carolina, Alabama, and Tennessee blacks. Unlike the Tennessee bureau, the Mississippi bureau merely heard testimony and gave legal advice to grieved men and women. The complaints filed by Grenada blacks in 1866 and 1867 in northeastern Mississippi were complaints filed primarily to protect close kin and friends. For example, on August 1, 1866, Charles (last name not available), said "his former employer drove him and his family off his place and threatened to shoot them if they returned." Five days later in another case, Jacob Campbell stated that his wife was tied up to a tree and whipped and lashed; "she being heavy with child at the time, he interfered and was beaten with fists and club by John and George Jordan." It goes on. There are about fifty pages in tiny script of such complaints recorded in the two-year period. Some of the complaints are the complaints of women; most are complaints of men.

Little in the prior experience in these Mississippi males should have shaped their consciousness in ways to distinguish them from most slave field hands in the South. In the content as well as the form of their complaints—and more significantly in their willingness to file their complaints—we find an acute awareness of paternal responsibility and familial obligation. Their behavior and that of other black men like them almost immediately upon emancipation casts up grave, if not final, doubt on the model for slave socialization which argues that the American or the North American slave as opposed to the Latin-American slave could serve neither as father nor husband. When freed these former Mississippi male slaves revealed in their behavior how quite ordinary rural black men responded to the abuse of close kin. Stanley Elkins argued convincingly that the personality traits and roles which developed over time among slave men and women could not change easily upon emancipation.

Emancipation did not transform the personalities of these Grenada male slaves, but their behavior as freedmen indicates to us quite a different process of socialization and adaptation to white men than that allowed by the model constructed by Elkins. Unless we are prepared to argue that these slaves' former owners socialized them to file protests, and that directly contradicts nature, reason, and even common sense, much more than what are called the basic variables—captivity, absolute power, and their effect on personality—shaped the behavior of these adult male husbands and fathers. These men had been born slaves and had grown up in a slave culture. Enslavement limited their behavior, but it had not shaped their personalities to accept such limitation as normal. Slave culture did not mirror the constraints of slave society, and that culture shaped the behavior of ordinary field hands as well as better-off slaves.

No evidence suggests that the Grenada blacks had been privileged slaves. Their names—Eli, Charles, Jacob, Campbell, Anderson, Kujo, Sam, Washington, Parnell, Daniel, Namen, and other such names— probably never again appeared in the historical records. They were neither conspicuous nor exceptional men. These were quite ordinary rural adult black husbands and fathers who revealed in their behavior in the immediate aftermath of emancipation that enslavement had not denied to them a powerful self-image as adult men. As slaves, they had learned of their duty to protect their wives and children from abuse and mistreatment. That awareness had come mostly from other slaves. They acted on these beliefs in 1865, 1866, and 1867 only because they had been freed. And their behavior reveals some of the powerful familial norms that had existed among them as enslaved men.

Genealogy of Afro-Americans

ALEX HALEY

In 1965 shortly after I had completed writing the *Autobiography of Malcolm X* and it had been published, I felt a sort of void or emptiness. While fiddling around in that state, I thought about the stories that my grandmother and various members of her generation had told me while visiting her home in Henning, Tennessee. It was from my grandmother's lips that I heard the story, which had come down across generations, about the slave family and the original "African." These bits of treasured oral history led to my research at the National Archives.

Actually, the story began in a little town called Henning, Tennessee. I grew up in that little town, which was fifty miles north of Memphis. Every summer grandmother would have as visitors family members of her general age range, the late forties or early fifties. They came from places that sounded pretty exotic to me—Dyersburg, Tennessee; Inkster, Michigan; and Saint Louis, Missouri. They included Cousin Georgia, Aunt Plus, and Aunt Liz. Every evening after the supper dishes were washed, they would go out on the front porch and sit in canebottomed rocking chairs, and I would always sit behind grandma's chair. Unless there was some particularly hot gossip that would overrule, they would talk about the selfsame thing—their parents who had lived in Alamance County, North Carolina. Their parents and grandparents were slaves and had lived there during the Civil War and emancipation. The family had come by wagon train from Alamance County, North Carolina, to the Murray plantation and finally to west Tennessee to the community called Blackfoot, which subsequently became Henning, Tennessee. It was these bits and pieces and patches of what I later learned was a long narrative history of the family that had been passed down, literally across generations.

MANIFEST of NEGROES, MULATTOS, and PERSONS OF COLOR, taken on board the *Barque Elizabeth* whereof *Alexander Joules* is Master, burthen *236* tons, to be transported to the port of *New Orleans* in the district of *Louisiana* for the purpose of being sold or disposed of as slaves, or to be held to service or labor.

NUMBER OF ENTRY	NAMES.	SEX. MALE.	FEMALE.	AGE.	HEIGHT. FEET.	INCHES.	COLOR.	OWNER OR SHIPPER'S NAME.	RESIDENCE.
1	Thomas Peck	·		21	5	11	Mulatto		
2	Isaac Pines	·		21	5	10	Blk		
3	Charles Pickell	·		17	5	8	Mulatto		
4	Perry Handy	·		22	5	7	Blk	Joseph S Donovan	
5	Hiram Wier	·		30	5	6	"	Shipper Baltimore	
6	George Brown	·		24	5	6	"		Md.
7	Horace Hall	·		30	5	5	"		
8	Cyrus Webster	·		18	5	4	Mulatto		
9	Caroline Wright		"	20	5	4	Blk		
10	Emly Tilghman		"	30	5	2	"		
11	Eveline Wilson		·	15	4	11	"		
12	Rachel Tilghman		·	28	4	10	"		
13	John Gray			38	5	8	·		
14	Charles Williams		"	22	5	5	·		
15	Hillery Alexander		"	26	5	4	"		
16	Caroline Pinkney		·	22	5	4	·		
17	Sally Plummer		"	6	3	8	·		
18	Mary Plummer		"	4	3	3	·		
19	Barbara Smith		"	15	5	1	·		
20	Sarah Hinson		·	16	5	2	·		
21	Ellen Stepney		·	24	5	3	·		
22	Benjn Stepney	·		infant			·		
23	John West		"	25	5	10	·		
24	Charles Bowley	·		25	5	9	·		
25	John Payton	·		19	5	7	·		
26	Albert Allen	·		17	5	5	·		
27	Charles Cooper			16	5	4	·		
28	Polly Gansbill		"	16	5	2	·		
29	Mary Thompson		"	18	5	1	·		
30	Thomas Colbert		·	20	5	7	·	Inspected & found Correct	
31	Patrick Selby		"	17	5	5	·		
32	Charlotte Harris		"	42	5	2	Brown		
33	Caroline Johnston		"	20	5	4	·		
34	Agnes Hicks		·	24	5	2	·		
35	Hanna Hicks		·	Infant			·		
36	Amelia Clark		"	17	5		·		
37	Martha Wing		"	17	5	3	Blk		
38	Charlotte Ann Ross		"	15	5	2	·		
39	Mary Jane Ones		"	12	4	7	Brown		
40	Ann Johnston		"	10	4	3	Blk		
41	Sarah Tute		"	10	4	4	Mulatto		
42	Albert Sexton			3	5	2	"		
43	Lewis Soll			30					

District of Baltimore, Port of Baltimore, *2d* day of *January* 1850.

Joseph S Donovan Shipper of the persons named and particularly described in the *above* manifest of *Negroes* and *Alexr Joiner* Master of the *Barque Elizabeth* do solemnly, sincerely, and truly swear, each of us to the best of our knowledge and belief that *the above described negroes* have not been imported in the United States since the first day of January, one thousand eight hundred and eight; and that under the Laws of the State of Maryland, *they are* held to service or labor as Slaves and *are* not entitled to freedom under these laws, at a certain time and after a known period of service.—SO HELP *us* GOD.

Sworn to this *2d* day of *January* 1850,

COLLECTOR.

John Van Wd

before *Joseph S Donovan*

Alexr Joiner

Manifest of ship arriving at the port of New Orleans from the port of Baltimore, January 1850. (RG 36, Bureau of Customs)

At that time, I did not understand their conversations. Sometimes they would talk about incidents that happened in these places. The furthermost person in the family history that they ever talked about was someone called "The African." Over the years, time and time again, I heard them repeat the African's story of his capture while he was chopping wood to make a drum and how he had been brought on a ship to "Naplis" where Marse John Waller of Spotsylvania County, Virginia, bought him and later sold him to his brother, William.

Although the African was now chattel, he resisted slavery. He fought to keep his African name until he was forced to accept the name Toby. He escaped several times but was recaptured each time. And the fourth time that he escaped, he was caught by a professional slave catcher and given the option of being castrated or having his foot amputated. The slave chose amputation, and his decision had great significance, for that act played a major role in the keeping of a narrative that was passed down across generations.

The African was now crippled and worth far less on the auction block. In the middle 1700s in Virginia, almost all slaves were sold at auction. A male slave in good condition would bring on the average about $750. At the end of every slave auction they would have what they called the scrap sale, and those who were incapacitated, ill, or otherwise not so valuable for market, would be sold generally for amounts of $100 or less in cash. Although this particular African managed to survive, he posed an economic question to his master. But despite the African's physical limitations, the master decided that he would be worth more kept on that plantation than he would be worth sold away for cash of less than $100. And that was how it happened that this particular African was kept on one plantation for quite a long period of time.

The African mated with a slave named Bell, the big house cook. Of that union was born a child named Kizzy. While Kizzy was still on the same plantation, the African passed a good deal of his heritage to her. He taught her the names for natural objects such as tree, rock, cow, sky, and so forth. The names that he told her were of his native tongue, but to the girl they were strange phonetic sounds. In time, with repetitive hearing, she could repeat them. He would point at a guitar and he would make a single sound as if it were spelled *ko*. And she came to know that *ko* was guitar in his terms. There were other strange phonetic sounds for other objects. Perhaps the most involved of these phonetic sounds was one which described the river (Mattaponi) contiguous to the plantation. Whenever this African would point out this river to his daughter Kizzy he would say to her

"Kamby Bolongo." And she came to know that *Kamby Bolongo* in his terms meant river.

When Kizzy was sixteen, she was sold to Tom Lea, the owner of a small North Carolina plantation. He became the father of her first child George, or Chicken George. When George was in his mid-teens, he was given the nickname Chicken George because he had learned to handle the master's fighting gamecocks.

At the age of eighteen, Chicken George married a slave girl named Matilda, who gave birth to seven children. One was named Tom who became an apprenticed blacksmith. He was sold in his mid-teens to a man named Murray who had a tobacco plantation in Alamance County, North Carolina. On this plantation Tom married a slave named Irene. Their youngest child was named Cynthia who was my maternal grandmother. I grew up in her home in Henning, Tennessee. The oral history of the family was passed down from generation to generation until I heard it on grandmother's front porch in Henning. And I wanted to know more.

In 1967 I visited the National Archives to research the Civil War and post-Civil War census tables for Alamance County, North Carolina. When I entered the Archives, I got a researcher's pass and went into a reading room. A young man at a desk asked me if he could help me, and I became mildly embarrassed because it seemed ridiculous to say that I was just curious about some ex-slaves that I had heard about from my grandparents and others. I just said that I wanted to see some Civil War and post-Civil War census tables for Alamance County, North Carolina.

This young research assistant was very helpful. He immediately showed me how to get the microfilm and in a few minutes I was at a microfilm reader ready to start. I turned the crank and the enlarged images of the materials on the film appeared on the screen and I began to see the names of the people. If I turned it slowly, the names went slowly; and I had the feeling of discovering people from yesteryears, from long, long ago. Then when I would turn it fast the names went by more briskly, and there was a mystique about it. I went through that sort of feeling for about three rolls of microfilm. But I did not find anything. By now I was really more taken with the physical motion of the film across the screen than I was with the contents, and I was pretty bored. So I just left the film there.

I was walking through the main reading room when I saw something that made a visual impression upon me. Generally people are relaxed in libraries. They lean back in the most comfortable positions that they can find. But in that library every single soul at every single table in that room was bent forward over the table engrossed in whatever was in their hands. And I saw the various records in their hands had the look of old rare documents. Some of them needed repairs, some needed to be reproduced, and some had already been reproduced. The scene gripped me and it dawned on me that perhaps 90 percent of the researchers were women and perhaps the same percentage were over sixty years of age. It seemed so very interesting that when people had lived most of their lives one of the things they wanted to know before they died was where they had come from.

That concept intrigued me so much that I returned to the microfilm reader. I began turning the microfilm again and I guess that I was on my eleventh roll when I suddenly looked down and read the names, written in that old longhand script, of my grandmother, my aunts, my great aunts, and others. It was not that I had not believed grandmother; you simply did not, not believe her. The point was that I had found a document, a government record, that said the same thing that grandmother and other members of the family had been saying for generations.

I began practically commuting between New York City, where I then lived, and Washington, D.C. I worked three months off and on in the National Archives, where a most interesting relationship developed. There may be a kind of mental telepathy among black people. One thing is certain, the National Archives black research assistants were so glad to know that someone was doing research in black history that they gave me a great deal of professional assistance. There was one fellow, who I would recognize to this day, who finally, indirectly as we will do sometimes, began to ask me questions and focus in on what I was doing. From that time on, when I put in a slip requesting materials, I got it twice as fast as anyone else in the Archives got theirs. It was a beautiful thing to watch. It also was a beautiful example of how starved black people are for good black history.

I discovered information that led me into the Library of Congress, where I began to work in county records, for further documentation. What I was doing all this time was little by little, piece by piece, facet by facet, documenting things that had always been a part of my family's history. Periodically, information that I found in a document coincided with what I knew of the oral history, which is such a strong part of the history of black people.

I began flying out to Kansas City to see Cousin Georgia, the youngest of the group that had sat and talked on grandmother's front porch when I was a kid. She was the only surviving member of that group. I would just walk into her house and she would start talking, like echoes from the past. She would say such things as: "Yeah, boy, they said this and that and the other.

The family lived in such and such county on such and such plantation. Old Marse so and so had them.'' Then I would research the records and I would find that the records said exactly the same thing that Cousin Georgia had said. I would make copies of some of the records and show them to her, and she would become indignant that I had ever thought that her accounts were not true in the first place. And so it went.

One thing led to another until finally I had been able to document every major facet of what had been, up to that time, the oral history of the family. It was at that point that I thought about writing a book on the United States side of the story, which I then knew pretty thoroughly. It was also at this point that the African sounds that had always been a part of the story came into play. There were not many of them. Just as others had told the story for years, Cousin Georgia now would tell how the African, as they always called him, would point to a guitar and say ''ko,'' or point to the Mattaponi River and say ''Kamby Bolongo.'' The African told his daughter that his name was Kinte and that he had been captured while chopping wood near his village. The fact that I had been able to corroborate or document so much of the oral history of the family in the United States made me feel that maybe it was not totally ridiculous to peer into the African side.

I set out to determine, if I could, what those African sounds meant and where they had originated. I began to go to the United Nation's lobby and stand around waiting for an African to pass. When one did, I tried to stop him and repeat the sounds to him. The Africans usually took a quick look at me and then kept going. They seemed startled to hear alleged African sounds from someone who had a Tennessee accent.

Having failed with that approach, I searched for a new way to get the meanings of those sounds. My very good friend, George Sims, a master researcher, suggested that I contact Dr. Jan Vansina of the University of Wisconsin, who was an expert in oral history. Vansina kindly acceded to my telephoned request for permission to visit him. There in his home in Madison, Wisconsin, he and some other scholars listened to the sounds and told me that they were of the Mandinka tongue, the language that is spoken by the Mandingo people. They guessed that *ko* meant kora in Mandingo. A *kora,* they said, was an old Mandinka musical instrument made of a large gourd covered with goat skin, with a long neck, a bridge, and twenty-one strings.

The pivotal step came next. He finally came to the most involved of the sounds that I had heard and had brought to him—*Kamby Bolongo.* Dr. Vansina and his colleagues told me, without question, in Mandinka, *Bolongo* meant river, preceded by *Kamby* it undoubtedly meant Gambia

River. That information gave me a place or area from which the African might have come, and I just had to get there.

It was Thursday morning when I heard those words; Monday morning I was in Africa. On Friday I had discovered that of the numerous African students in this country, there were a few from that very small country called The Gambia, West Africa. The one who was nearest was a fellow who was attending Hamilton College in Clinton, New York. I had gone to the campus and practically snatched Ebou Manga out of his economics class. We had flown out of New York that Friday night and had traveled through the night to Dakar, Senegal. There we took a light plane that flew to a little airstrip called Yundum, where monkeys had to be chased from the landing strip before the plane could land. We hired a van and went into the small city of Bathurst, the capital of The Gambia. Ebou Manga's father assembled a group of about eight men, members of the government, who came into the patio of the hotel. They sat in a kind of a semicircle as I told them the history that had come down across the family to my grandmother and thence to me.

When I finished the story, their initial response was "well, of course *Kamby Bolongo* would mean Gambia River." These Africans reacted to the sound "Kin-tay," a mere two-syllable sound that I had brought them, without the slightest comprehension that it had any particular significance. They said, "There may be some significance in that your forefather stated that his name was Kin-tay." They continued, "Our oldest villages tend to be named for those families which founded those villages centuries ago." And then they sent for a little map and they said, "Look, here is the village of Kinte-Kundah. And not too far from it is the village of Kinte-Kundah-Janneh-Ya."

There in The Gambia for the first time I became aware of how black Africans keep their history. It is kept by old men called *griots,* who are in effect walking, living archives of oral history. They are the old men who, from their teen years, have been part of a line of men who tell the stories as told since the time of their forefathers, literally down across centuries. A line of *griots* might consist of an old man of seventy years of age, and after him successively younger men like sixty, fifty, forty, thirty, twenty, and a teenage boy. Each line of *griots* is an expert in the story of a major family clan and another line of *griots* another clan, and so forth.

The stories are narrated, not verbatim, but essentially in the same way they have been told down across time since the forefathers. The way the *griots* are trained is that the teenage boy is exposed to the story of a major clan for forty or fifty years before becoming the incumbent *griot.* Such a feat astounds us in our society because we have become so accustomed to the crutch of the printed word that we have almost forgotten the extent to which the human memory is capable of being trained—as it is in Africa—to be a repository of history.

I finally came to realize that for almost any black American who has a few clues like the African name of an ancestor and the approximate time and place of their sailing, there is the possibility for successful genealogical research. It is not improbable that in the back country of black West Africa there is a wizened old *griot* who literally could tell the ancestral clan from which the black American came.

The Africans could not help me much more at that time, so I returned to New York. It was not long before I received a letter explaining their discovery of a *griot* who could help me. I rushed back to The Gambia, where I had to organize a safari to go into the back country. I entered the back country village and was introduced to Kebba Kanga Fofana, an old *griot* who told me in meticulous details the history of the Kinte clan.

Fofana said that the Kinte clan began in Old Mali. Traditionally, the Kinte people were blacksmiths, potters, and weavers. A branch of the clan moved into the country called Mauretania. Kairaba Kunta Kinte, a son of the Kinte Clan, left the country of Mauretania and settled in a village called Pakali N'Ding in The Gambia. He later moved to another village called Jiffarong, and later went to the Juffure Village. In that village, he married a Mandinka maiden named Yaisa. Of that marriage, two sons were born, Janneh and Saloum.

In a second marriage, a son named Omoro was born to Kairaba Kunta Kinte. The three sons grew up in the Juffure Village. The youngest of the sons stayed in the village until he had 30 rains [years] and then he married Binta Kebba. They had four sons—Kunta, Lamin, Suwadu, and Madi. The *griot* stated, ''About the time the king's soldiers came, the youngest of the sons went away from the village to chop wood and was seen never again.'' While growing up in Henning, Tennessee, and practically all my life, I had heard the story of the African who said that his name was Kunta Kinte and that he was kidnapped while chopping wood near the Juffure Village. And now it had been put together, both the American and African side of the story.

From the time I was a child, grandmother had always said that the ship that brought Kinte to this country had sailed to ''Naplis.'' The only place in the world that she could have meant was Annapolis, Maryland. I knew specifically where that slave came from, so obviously some ship had come from that area of the Gambia River and sailed to Maryland. I went to

REPORT and MANIFEST of the LADING of the *Sloop Polly* — — burthen *Thirty Six & Seventy two* 95 Tons, American built, from *the Isle of Goree* being the Port from whence she last sailed, — Master during the Voyage *Joshua Smith* - the present Master, and is owned by *Cyprian Sterry of Providence Rhode Island*

Marks	Numbers	Contents of each Package, &c. or Quantity, if stowed loose.	By whom shipped.	Where destined.	To whom consigned.	Port or Place where laden.
	1 - 40	Forty Slaves	Isaac Gorham	Samuel in Georgia	Robert Watts	The River of Gam
		Stores				
		One Barrel Beef				
		One half Barrel Pork				
		Two Barrels Corn				
		Ten Gallons Rum				

Manifest of the Sloop Polly *carrying slaves from the Gambia River in Africa to Providence, Rhode Island, September 1795.* (RG 36, Bureau of Customs)

England to get some documentary evidence of such a ship because these events happened while Maryland was still an English colony.

I began to search for the records of ships that had sailed from Africa to this country. There were cartons of records that had never been opened of slave ships, of ships in general, that moved two centuries ago. In the seventh week of an almost traumatizing search, I found the name of the ship that sailed from the Gambia River to Gravesend, England. She was the eighteenth ship on the list, and was called the *Lord Ligonier,* a 170 ton vessel under the command of a Thomas Davies. On September 13, 1766, she reached the Gambia River and for several months she lay there gathering a cargo that included 3,265 elephant tusks, 3,700 pounds of beeswax, 800 pounds of cotton, 32 ounces of gold, and 140 slaves. On Sunday, July 5, 1767, she set sail for Annapolis, Maryland.

Having found out what cargo the *Lord Ligonier* had when she left Africa, I now returned to the United States to try to find out what cargo she had when she arrived in Annapolis. I began searching tax records—the one kind of record that exists in some form back to the time of Christ—to see what cargo taxes the *Lord Ligonier* had paid. She arrived in Annapolis after a voyage of about five thousand miles that took two months, three weeks, and two days. She had almost the same cargo, but only 98 of the 140 slaves

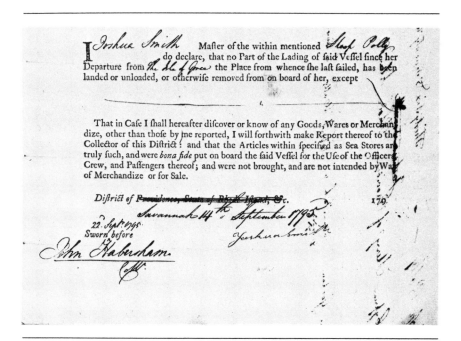

she had sailed with survived the voyage; the number of slaves who died enroute was about average for slave ships. That same ship left Gravesend, England, with thirty-six crewmembers and arrived in Annapolis, with only eighteen alive. So they lost proportionately more crewmembers than they lost slaves. But slaves had value. The crewmembers had no value once they had gotten the slaves on the ships. In some instances, members of the crews were encouraged to commit suicide so they would not be around at the end of the voyage to collect the wages due them. Slavery was indeed a totally brutalizing system for both the captives and the captors.

After searching the *Maryland Gazette,* I found the ad that listed the slave ship, *Lord Ligonier*. The ad stated: "the *Lord Ligonier* with Captain Davies, had just arrived with a cargo of choice healthy slaves to be sold at Meg's Wharf . . . and the agent of the ship was John Riddout.'' (A descendant of his has written me seeking forgiveness for her ancestors' connection with slavery.)

Now that I had found documentation for the ship that brought the African from the Gambia River to Annapolis, I wanted to find written evidence linking him to his Virginia owner. I knew that most transactions involving slaves were legal matters. So I went to Richmond, Virginia, to obtain the legal deeds. I found a deed that was dated September 5, 1768, transferring goods between the two brothers John and William Waller of Spotsylvania County, Virginia. On the second page in this fairly long deed were the words "and also one Negro slave named Toby." So that was the documentation of my family's lineage, down to the legal deeds.

I hope that this paper will project a worldwide correction of a fallacy that plagues not just black history, but the history of all peoples: History has been written and stored predominantly by the winners. More stories of black family lineage will spread an awareness that black history is not just some euphemistic cry on the part of a people trying to make some spurious case for themselves, but that black history is a matter of disciplined, documented, dedicated truth. The National Archives has opened the door to researchers, and more important, reemphasized that black history must become a viable part of the history of this nation.

Discussion Summary

Okon Edet Uya of Howard University began the discussion with the comment that oral history is always properly kept, but it is not always properly collected. He then posed the following questions: Is there an overriding concern with proving through indices of primary families the existence of a particular form of family life among black Americans? What, if any, research is being done on the extended family?

Andrew Billingsley of Howard University replied that he did not define "family" in his limited presentation and that he did not attempt to prove the existence of the nuclear European family among slaves from Africa. In examining the records, he had found various patterns of structured relationships and is now convinced that there is a great deal of continuity between the forms of family life practiced by blacks in Africa and the Afro-American forms of family life practiced even during slavery. He said that he would continue to search for patterns of intimate relationships that exist among blacks.

Billingsley concluded that both he and Prof. Benjamin Quarles were interested in records and oral history as sources to study the various patterns of structured relationships. They are convinced that there is a continuity between the forms of family life known in Africa and the forms of family life known among the slaves.

Herbert G. Gutman of the City College of New York also responded to Uya's question by stating that about three-fourths of the forced African emigrants were brought to the mainland colonies between 1720 and 1770, but we know very little about their family life during that period. During those decades and for several generations afterward, there was a great diffusion of cultures and family systems, out of which came the slave family which is not necessarily nuclear. He explained that a study of the plantation community would have to be done with something other than a marriage register. It must be done with other kinds of evidence that would show "the development under slavery of extraordinarily extended kin structures."

Gutman concluded that until more is known of the African family and kinship structures that influenced the Afro-American component in the eighteenth century, he was prepared to call them Afro-American kinship structures developed by slaves which may have very significant African components.

Vincent Harding of the Institute of the Black World, Atlanta, Georgia, felt that Gutman had missed an important point in analyzing the responsibility slave men took for their families. Even as slaves, black men died protecting their families or they gave their lives in avenging assaults on their families.

Gutman replied that emancipation did not suddenly create this concern and sense of responsibility among slaves for their families, it simply opened up the possibility for acting it out. Emancipation widened the boundaries in which black women and men could act, but it did not alter their ideas of how to act. Slavery had placed limitations on their behavior only. He concluded that one should study the slave culture both during slavery and immediately after emancipation.

In response to a question about Ulrich B. Phillips's views on slavery and blacks, Gutman said that if further research led to the conclusion that slavery was less harsh than it is now believed to have been, the question would become, "why was it less harsh?" He contended, though, that Phillips had no conception of slaves and the slave culture and that his conception of slavery as a benign institution was the imposition of his personal racial beliefs on the slave experience.

Gutman said that some contemporary historians are attempting to give long-overdue recognition to the powerful role slaves played in shaping their own lives. He called Professor Stampp's book a good one, but pointed out that Stampp, Elkins, and Phillips were really concerned about the very appropriate question of what American slavery did to its African captives. However, historians are now concerned about the other side of the equation; they want to understand what happened to the enslaved after acculturation. In answering that question, Gutman asserted, historians can really find out how the system worked and not worry about whether it was more or less harsh.

Billingsley responded to the same question with the observation that his research did not necessarily support the view that slavery was not as harsh as others had said it was. He also noted that if we find that black people have survived the worst holocaust known to people, that not only tells us something about the nature of the holocaust, it also tells us something about black people. And if we find that there developed during slavery stable patterns of love relationships and affection and caring, that tells us even more about the nature of the system and about blacks as a people. Billingsley does not conclude, however, that these stable patterns rendered the system of slavery less harsh. He said that his research leads to the conclusion that "the capacity to survive and love was stronger than that system and that among black people that capacity won out once in a while, and that is what we see."

VI

Assessment and Prospects

The National Archives and Records Service: An Evaluation of Afro-American Resources

JOHN W. BLASSINGAME

The National Archives of the United States is such a young institution that anyone familiar with it must be awed by the services it provides. Increasingly, scholars are using the voluminous records it contains. Significantly, the Association for the Study of Negro Life and History (ASNLH) [now known as the Association for the Study of Afro-American Life and History] has been in the forefront of those urging students to explore these materials. In 1937 James Mock and Carl Lokke read an address on the subject at the ASNLH annual meeting and twelve years later Roland McConnell made an appeal for greater use of the research materials available in the National Archives.

Such appeals appeared earlier in the *Journal of Negro History* because of the special barriers to research black historians encountered. The paucity of records relating to blacks, the inaccessibility of much of this material in state and college libraries which barred black scholars, and the lack of objectivity in many "white" sources, forced many black scholars to consider using the National Archives in the 1930s, and after that time.

The records in the archives, created in the ordinary course of government business, are extensive and often include the names and activities of thousands of blacks. There is, in effect, less conscious distortion of fact than is true of most other records created by whites. This is not to say that the records do not reflect the prejudice of federal employees and consistent discrimination by the government. There is, however, one distinction in this regard. Since the records represent the internal communication of various agencies, the prejudices and discriminatory plans and activities are presented candidly.

In this volume, most writers have focused on the kinds of materials and services that are available rather than their limitations. The Freedmen's Bureau, military, and Justice Department records were mentioned most often by contributors to this volume as especially valuable. The case studies based on these and other records were illuminating because they demonstrated the kind of history one can write when relying on the National Archives. From an informational standpoint, the volume has revealed many facets of the National Archives. We have learned a great deal about the positive features of the Archives and gained some superficial knowledge of the way it operates. More importantly, we have restricted our research papers almost exclusively to the status quo. We have gained little appreciation for, or knowledge of, the way policies regarding Afro-Americans have evolved over time. We have little sense of what is being planned for the future.

Okon Edet Uya and Alex Haley raised some significant questions about the nature of federal archives and cautioned us against viewing their contents as the new panacea. But beyond this, few of the papers dealt with some of the fundamental issues relative to federal archives. While Robert Clarke and the National Archives staff have tried to educate us about what is available, those who have presented papers have done little to educate the Archives about what we *need* and how the services must be improved.

Some fundamental questions were raised by those who did not present papers at this conference. Vincent Harding raised many of these questions, and underlying them was a query which nagged at many of us: Who decides what records are preserved? From the archivist's viewpoint, one of the most important aspects of this question is how much material should be destroyed. Our government runs on paper and there would never be enough space to save all of it. Still, one has to wonder if the paper shredders do not sometimes run too long in Washington. At one time I had complete faith in the Archives' ability to appraise the historical worth of federal records. But then I found that the staff once decided to destroy the social schedules of the census, then gave them to the Daughters of the American Revolution (DAR), which gave them to Duke University, which several years later permitted the Archives to microfilm them. Understandably, I have had some difficulty in restoring my faith in the appraising skills of the staff since then.

In spite of all of the promise inherent in the Archives and detailed in a number of the papers presented in this volume, there are also many problems. Given the extensive sources available and the relative lack of them for the study of black history, much more must be done to facilitate a greater and more diverse use of the National Archives. Until recently, however, the Archives has done relatively little to promote research on Afro-Americans. First, few blacks have been hired for or promoted to responsible positions. Since 1960 I have listened repeatedly to talented and concerned blacks complain about discrimination in promotion and their consequent low morale. Every time I found a series of records that was not indexed properly I was embittered because it was a direct reflection of this waste of talent and interest. The rareness of white staff members who are both skilled and interested in research on Afro-Americans and the difficulties of changing negative perceptions of the subject would seem to indicate that the shortest route to upgrading archival services in this area is to increase the number of blacks on the staff.

One general shortcoming of the Archives is so acute in relation to the records of Afro-Americans that it deserves special attention. All too often the general records are so poorly indexed that they are practically inaccessible. The checklists of many record groups that are of special interest in studying blacks must be revised. These include the Freedmen's Bureau, comptroller of the currency, adjutant general, attorney general, Fair Employment Practice Commission, and congressional records. The importance of these checklists cannot be overestimated. The current checklists are so inadequate that many of us are frustrated in our research.

In 1963 I received a grant to study the largest all-black military unit in American history, the Twenty-fifth Army Corps, which was organized during the Civil War. I spent several days going through checklists and could not find any record that the corps ever existed. As I got up to leave the office, I met Sara Jackson and told her of my problem. She immediately led me to the stacks where we found dozens of uncatalogued books on the Twenty-fifth Army Corps. As a result of this experience, I have never completely accepted the idea that the Central Research Office is an advancement over the old system of permitting students to go directly to the office in charge of the records for each agency. In the Archives, as in any repository, contact with those individuals with the most comprehensive knowledge of records is indispensable for the researchers. But, still, there is a need for adequate guides to the materials.

Even when all of the records of an agency are included in a checklist, it is sometimes difficult to utilize them. Generally, the records are described according to the functions of the agency and reveal only incidental matters of race. These incidentals are, however, of primary concern to students of Afro-American life and should be described in greater detail. There are many ways of doing this.

First, the Archives should expand its cooperation with American University in archival use to include Howard University and the Association for the Study of Negro Life and History. The ASNLH could provide technical assistance to the Archives in specific subject areas and in establishing priorities in preparing guides. Howard University's history department and library could provide students who are interested in certain subjects and people to help supervise them in collecting materials, which could then be used by the Archives staff in preparing research guides. Both the association and Howard have been engaged in collecting and preserving the records of Afro-Americans so much longer than the Archives that all scholars would benefit from their close and continuous cooperation.

Second, the Archives should call upon all scholars who have done research on blacks to describe their findings in each record group that they have used. In this case, the files of the Central Research Office could be utilized to compile a list of the scholars. Robert Clarke would be the logical person to conduct the survey. I am convinced that most scholars would be enthusiastic about such an effort.

Finally, something must be done immediately to revise the general description of records in the Archives relating to Afro-Americans (*A Guide to Documents in the National Archives for Negro Studies,* compiled by Paul Lewinson), which was published in 1947. It seems that Clarke could do this revision by requesting that each person in charge of a record group mentioned in the original edition furnish a more detailed description of the materials. This is not an easy task; it requires unusual cooperation among several agencies. From my work with several college faculties, I would hazard a guess that it would only succeed with the active support of the archivist of the United States.

Edgar Toppin has ably described the activities and plans of the National Historical Publications and Records Commission (NHPRC). In order to understand and appreciate those activities, they must be placed in historical perspective. Before discussing NHPRC, however, I would like to preface my evaluation with a few observations and disclaimers. Any grant-awarding agency creates enemies of all those applicants who are turned down, and sometimes only lukewarm friends of those whose projects are funded at less than 100 percent. In my association with both the Booker T. Washington and the Frederick Douglass papers, I have been encouraged by NHPRC. Needless to say, I have not yet reached that 100 percent funding level. Still, I consider myself a friend of the commission. But my remarks are not directed to that. Instead, I would like to reconsider the reasons for the small number of editing projects on Afro-Americans supported by NHPRC.

The inattention of NHPRC to the promotion of research on Afro-Americans is entirely consistent with the traditional approach of government agencies and private foundations regarding blacks. The real support of editing projects concerning blacks by these institutions has been somewhat less than minute. Frequently, the lack of support has been almost unbelievable. All Americans should be ashamed of the fact that one of their greatest scholars, W.E.B. Du Bois, could obtain no consistent support for his encyclopedia of the Negro project. With all of the funds available in the United States at that time, Du Bois received his only real support for the project from the Ghanaian government shortly before he died. Du Bois did not complete the project. For those scholars who do not wish to go into exile in order to obtain money to edit the papers of Afro-Americans, the record of NHPRC is bleak. According to a survey made a few years ago by Jesse Lemisch, the NHPRC was dedicated from its origin to publishing "the papers of great white men."

Although it would be easy to place all of the blame on NHPRC, the major responsibility rests with the predominantly white historical guild. After all, the original list of projects was based on a survey of American historians. Women and blacks were so invisible, so inconsequential in the minds of white scholars in the 1950s, that only one black and four women were included among the 112 projects first noted by NHPRC. There were no blacks included in the projects that received top priority for funding. Because of the blindness of white scholars, NHPRC became saddled with an "exclusively for white men" list of priorities. This, in addition to inadequate funding, has prevented greater inclusion of projects on blacks, even when several members of the commission staff pushed for it.

All scholars interested in Afro-American research must also bear part of the blame for the shortcomings of NHPRC. Now, and in the future, we must support Professor Toppin and his committee. We must begin to write our representatives in Congress to obtain more money to support editing projects involving Afro-Americans.

The National Archives Conference on Federal Archives as Sources for Research on Afro-Americans has done much to indicate the potentials for research on Afro-Americans in the National Archives. It would be easy to focus on those possibilities. But I do not believe that they will be realized unless there is some systematic effort to deal with the problems that we all know exist. The entire National Archives staff should be commended for having the courage to hold a conference that offers constructive criticisms on Afro-American research and, at the same time, celebrates the progress that has been made in this area.

APPENDIX
BIOGRAPHICAL SKETCHES
INDEX

Appendix: Gallery of Selected Archival Documents Relating to Afro-Americans

The National Archives and Records Service administers the permanently valuable, noncurrent records of the federal government. These archival holdings date from the days of the Continental Congresses to the present, and include documents from almost every federal agency, both civil and military.

Among the valuable records of the federal government are documents that contain information on the history of Afro-Americans. The following records are select examples of such documents. They represent only a few of the agencies of the government, and their contents should not be considered inclusive. These records are presented in the hope that they, too, will encourage inquiries and promote even greater use of federal archives as sources for studies on Afro-American history.

OVERLEAF:

Passport application. These applications may be used to obtain or verify vital statistics and physical descriptions. When the passport covers more than one member of a family, the application sometimes includes names, ages, and birth dates of the other family members. This application is from George Washington Williams, a Civil War veteran and distinguished historian who traveled in Africa and Europe. (RG 59, Department of State)

173

No. _12282_   Issued _June 30, 1884_

UNITED STATES OF AMERICA.

~~State of~~ _District of Columbia_ ⎫
                                      ⎬ ss.
County of _Washington_ ⎰

I _George W. Williams_ , do swear that I was born in
the _Pennsylvania_ , on or about the _16th_ day
of _October 1847_ ; that I am a **Native and Loyal Citizen of the United States,**
and about to travel abroad _____

Sworn to before me this _30th_ day
of _June_ , 1884   _Geo. W. Williams_

Newton Benedict
Notary Public.

I, _____ , do swear that I am acquainted
with the above-named _____ , and with the facts stated
by _____ and that the same are true to the best of my knowledge and belief.
Sworn to before me this _____ day
of _____ , 18___

_____
Notary Public.

DESCRIPTION OF _George W. Williams_

Age, _36_ years.   Mouth, _large_
Stature, _5_ feet _8 1/4_ inches, Eng. Chin, _broad_
Forehead, _high_   Hair, _dark_
Eyes, _dark hazel_   Complexion, _dark_
Nose, _medium_   Face, _oval_

I, _George W. Williams_ , do solemnly swear that I will support, protect,
and defend the Constitution and Government of the United States against all enemies, whether domestic or foreign;
and that I will bear true faith, allegiance, and loyalty to the same, any ordinance, resolution, or law of any State,
Convention, or Legislature to the contrary notwithstanding; and further, that I do this with a full determination,
pledge, and purpose, without any mental reservation or evasion whatsoever; and further, that I will well and faithfully
perform all the duties which may be required of me by law: So help me God.

Geo. W. Williams

SWORN to before me this _30th_ day of _June_ , 1884.

Newton Benedict

Applicant desires passport sent to following address :

_____

_____

174

Foreign incoming manifests. Since the importation of slave property was legal until 1808, some foreign manifests listed slaves as cargo of the incoming ships. Shown here is a manifest of the *Schooner Dolphin* that sailed ca. 1800 from the port of Goree in Africa to the United States. (RG 36, U.S. Customs Service)

Slave manifest. Masters of ships sailing between domestic ports submitted lists of the slaves on board. The manifests provide information about individual slaves and the domestic slave trade. (RG 36, U.S. Customs Service)

PETITION.

To the Commissioner of Patents:

The Petition of *Elijah McCoy, of Ypsilanti Washtenaw County, Michigan*

Respectfully Represents That your petitioner *has* invented a new and useful improvement in *lubricating cylinders* which *he* verily believe has never before been known or used prior to the invention thereof by your petitioner ; *he* therefore pray that Letters Patent of the United States may be granted to *him* therefor, vesting in *me* and *my* legal representatives the exclusive right to the same, upon the terms and conditions expressed in the act of Congress in that case made and provided, *and* having paid Fifteen Dollars into the Treasury, and complied with the other provisions of the said act. Your petitioner would further pray that **Alexander & Mason**, of Washington, D. C., be recognized as *his* sole lawful solicitors and advocates for *me* and in *my* name, to solicit and advocate, amend this application, to receive the Patent if granted, and in all other respects to do all your petitioner could do if personally acting in the premises.

Name of Applicant.   *Elijah McCoy*

To all whom it may concern:

BE IT KNOWN, That *Elijah McCoy*

of *Ypsilanti* , in the County of *Washtenaw* and in the State of *Michigan* have invented certain new and useful improvements in *a lubricator for cylinders*

and do hereby declare that the following is a full, clear and exact description thereof, reference being had to the accompanying drawings and to the letters of reference marked thereon, making a part of this specification.

Documents selected from a patent application file. Afro-Americans have contributed to the development and the well-being of their country with numerous inventions. A typical patent file includes documents such as these from one of Elijah McCoy's many successful patent applications. (RG 241, Patent Office)

176

In Testimony That _I_ *claim the foregoing* _I_ *have hereunto set* _my_ hand and seal this _28th_ day of _June_ 187_2_.

Witness { *E. X. Allen*
{ *Albert Crumm*

Inventor { *Elijah McCoy*

OATH.

COUNTY OF *Washtenaw*

STATE OF *Michigan*

On this _28_ day of _June_ 1872, before me, the subscriber, duly qualified to administer oaths, personally appeared the within named _Elijah McCoy_ and made solemn oath that _he_ verily believe_s_ _himself_ to be the original and first inventor of the within described _lubricator for cylinders_ and that _he does_ not know or believe that the same was ever before known or used; and that _he is a_ citizen of the United States.

Edward X. Allen
Notary Public
Washtenaw County
Michigan

The applicant will execute these papers as follows : Sign the Petition and Specification upon the lines printed for that purpose, affix and cancel a 50 cent Revenue Stamp as indicated, then make oath (or affirmation) before a J. P., or other qualified officer.

ALEXANDER & MASON,

SOLICITORS OF

AMERICAN AND EUROPEAN PATENTS

AND

COUNSELLORS AT PATENT LAW,

No. 460 SEVENTH STREET.　　　　OPPOSITE U. S. PATENT OFFICE,

WASHINGTON, D. C.

177

E. McCOY.

Improvement in Lubricators for Steam-Engines.

No. 130,305.

Patented Aug. 6, 1872.

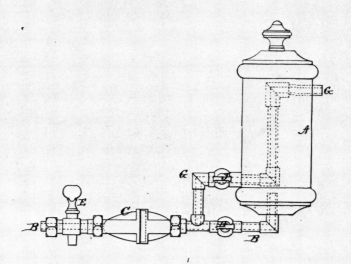

Witnesses:
Jas. M. Calchinson
C. L. Euert.

Inventor.
Elijah McCoy.
per
Attorneys.

178

UNITED STATES PATENT OFFICE.

ELIJAH McCOY, OF YPSILANTI, MICHIGAN.

IMPROVEMENT IN LUBRICATORS FOR STEAM-ENGINES.

Specification forming part of Letters Patent No. **130,305**, dated August 6, 1872.

To all whom it may concern:

Be it known that I, ELIJAH McCOY, of Ypsilanti, in the county of Washtenaw and in the State of Michigan, have invented certain new and useful Improvements in a Lubricator for Cylinders; and do hereby declare that the following is a full, clear, and exact description thereof, reference being had to the accompanying drawing and to the letters of reference marked thereon, making a part of this specification.

The nature of my invention consists in the construction and arrangement of a "steam-cylinder lubricator," as will be hereinafter more fully set forth.

In order to enable others skilled in the art to which my invention appertains to make and use the same, I will now proceed to describe its construction and operation, referring to the annexed drawing, which represents a side elevation of my invention.

A represents the vessel in which the oil is contained, and from the bottom of which a pipe, B, leads to the steam-chest. This pipe is, at a suitable point, provided with a globe or reservoir, C. Between the vessel A and the globe or reservoir C is a stop-cock, D, in the pipe B, and in the same pipe, between the globe and the steam-chest, is another stop-cock, E. A steam-pipe, G, passes from the dome or boiler down through the vessel and connects with the oil-pipe B at the glove or reservoir C, or at any point between the same

and the valve D. In the steam-pipe G, after it leaves the vessel A, is a stop-cock, J. One of these oilers is to be placed on each side of the smoke-arch directly opposite the cylinders, and the various stop-cocks should be so connected with levers or rods that they can be operated simultaneously by a single rod in the engineer's cab. When the engine is working the stop-cocks E and J are closed and the stop-cock D opened, allowing the oil to pass into the globe or reservoir C. The steam being in the pipe G prevents the oil from congealing in cold weather in the vessel A. When the cylinder is to be oiled the stop-cocks E and J are opened and D closed. Steam passing from the boiler or dome through the pipe G forces the oil out of the globe or reservoir C into the cylinder.

Having thus fully described my invention, what I claim as new, and desire to secure by Letters Patent, is—

The combination of the vessel A, oil-pipe B with reservoir C and stop-cocks D E, and the steam-pipe G with the stop-cock J, all constructed and arranged substantially as and for the purposes herein set forth.

In testimony that I claim the foregoing I have hereunto set my hand this 28th day of June, 1872.

ELIJAH McCOY.

Witnesses:
E. P. ALLEN,
ALBERT GROVE.

OVERLEAF:

A muster roll of a volunteer military organization. Muster rolls list the names of persons in a particular military unit. They also provide some insight into the military life of a soldier by listing information on unauthorized absences, confinements, and transfers. (RG 94, Adjutant General's Office)

NO.	NAMES. PRESENT AND ABSENT. (Privates in alphabetical order)	RANK.	JOINED FOR SERVICE AND ENROLLED AT GENERAL RENDEZVOUS. COMMENCEMENT OF FIRST PAYMENT BY TIME. When.	Where.	By Whom.	Period.	MUSTERED INTO SERVICE. When.	Where.	By Whom.	
1	George D H Guest	1st Lieut	25 Sept 63	3d Hudson Ja		3 Yrs	26 Sept 1863	3d Hudson	Maj J C Ward	
2	Curtis Y Prall	2d	...	...		"	6 Oct	...	...	
1	Francis Catherine	Sergt	29 May 63	New Orleans	Capt H L Foy	"	27 Sept 63	New Orleans	Maj Giddings	
2	John Anderson	5th	"	"	"		"	"	"	"	
3	August Walter	3d	2d Spt	"	"	"	"	"	"	"	
4	Adam Patterson	4th	15 "	"	"	"	"	"	"	"	
5	Jules Daily	1st	9 "	"	"	"	"	"	"	"	
6	Harrison Davis	1st Cpl	9d	"	"	"	"	"	"	"	
7	Jean St Parrien	2d	15 "	"	"	"	"	"	"	"	
8	Walter Fripp	3d	12 Dec	Columbia	"	"	12 Dec	Lafourche	Col Stafford	
9	Charles Marius	4th	29 Sept	New Orleans	"	"	27 Spt	New Orleans	Maj Giddings	
11	Francis Valentine	5th	"	"	"	"	"	"	"	"	
1	John Sidney	Musn	29 May	"	"	"	"	"	"	"	
2	Jules S Fuller	"	15 Spt	"	"	"	"	"	"	"	
1	Augustin Jacquins	Privt	2d Spt	"	"	"	"	"	"	"	
2	Brune Richard	"	22 "	"	"	"	"	"	"	"	
3	Batt William	"	9 "	"	"	"	"	"	"	"	
4	Bradford Henry	"	15 Dec	Lafourche La	"	"	15 Dec	Lafourche	Col Stafford	
5	Bradley Frank	"	"	"	"	"	"	"	"	"	
6	Batest Louis	"	2d "	"	"	"	2d "	"	"	"	
7	Compant Auguste	"	"	"	"	"	"	"	"	"	
8	Baptiste Jules	"	9 Sept	New Orleans	"	"	27 Sept	New Orleans	Maj Giddings	
9	Clement Henry	"	"	"	"	"	"	"	"	"	
10	Crawford William	"	"	"	"	"	"	"	"	"	
11	Chaland Emile	"	"	"	"	"	"	"	"	"	
12	Davis Janvier J	"	"	"	"	"	"	"	"	"	
13	Fletcher Ferdinand	"	"	"	"	"	"	"	"	"	
14	Fernande Francis	"	"	"	"	"	"	"	"	"	
15	Fernande Henry	"	"	"	"	"	"	"	"	"	
16	Guillot Arthur	"	"	"	"	"	"	"	"	"	
17	Gregoir Gabriel	"	"	"	"	"	"	"	"	"	
18	Hagan Charles	"	"	"	"	"	"	"	"	"	
19	Hall Henry	"	"	"	"	"	"	"	"	"	
20	Hall Samuel	"	31 March 63	Baton Rouge	"	"	30 April 63	Baton Rouge	Col Stafford	
21	Joseph Joe	"	18 Sept 63	New Orleans	"	"	27 Spt 63	New Orleans	Maj Giddings	
22	John Richard	"	21 March	Baton Rouge	"	"	30 April 63	Baton Rouge	Col Stafford	
23	Johnson John	"	18 Sept 63	New Orleans	"	"	27 Spt 63	New Orleans	Maj Giddings	
24	Julien Eugene	"	21 March	Baton Rouge	"	"	30 April 63	Baton Rouge	Col Stafford	
25	Julien Gustave	"	14 Aug 63	Port Hudson	Lieut Haff	"	14 Aug	Port Hudson	Maj J C Ward	
26	John Anderson	"	"	"	"	"	"	"	"	"	
27	Lee John	"	18 Sept 63	New Orleans	Capt H L Foy	"	27 Spt 63	New Orleans	Maj Giddings	
28	Lee Auguste	"	"	"	"	"	"	"	"	"	
29	Mathieu Antoine	"	"	"	"	"	"	"	"	"	
30	Mathieu L Henry	"	23 Aug	"	"	"	"	"	"	"	
31	Meta Henry	"	18 Sept	"	"	"	"	"	"	"	
32	Patterson Joseph	"	"	"	"	"	"	"	"	"	
33	Pentoiseau Victor	"	"	"	"	"	"	"	"	"	
34	Shepperd Sam	"	"	"	"	"	"	"	"	"	
35	Strong Benjamin	"	"	"	"	"	"	"	"	"	
36	Singis Henry	"	5 Dec	Lafourche	"	"	15 Dec	Lafourche	Col Stafford	
37	Thompson Joseph	"	18 Sept	New Orleans	"	"	27 Sept	New Orleans	Maj Giddings	
38	Thomas William	"	"	"	"	"	"	"	"	"	
39	Vollen Louis	"	"	"	"	"	"	"	"	"	
40	Ward George	"	"	"	"	"	"	"	"	"	
41	Walter Billing	"	"	"	"	"	"	"	"	"	

Transferred

Capt M Converse   1st Lieut 31 March 63 Port Hudson   3 Yrs 1 April 4 Port Hudson Maj J C Ward

Infantry   Regiment of *La Corps d'Afrique*   , United States Army,

1863 , when last mustered, to the *Twentyninth* day of *February*   *1864* .

Time.	NAMES. PRESENT.	
1863	George Mc Guest Eudiss G. Pratt	Never been paid. Was detached from Company G and assigned to be Company B Co R.S. 161 by Regimental Orders 38 & 10 and is entitled to pay for responsibility of arms &c from that date. Entitled to pay for responsibility of arms &c from Nov 8th as Co RS 161 1863.
"	John Andrews	Absent without leave since February 24th 1864
"	Alfred Andre	
"	Oscar Bentoiseau	
"	Jules Frits	
"	Harrison Davis	
"	Martin Fiss	Absent without leave since February 24th 1864
"	Charles Sharius	
"	Francois Valentine	
4	John Sidney	On detached duty as Drummer at Hd Qrs 6th Brigade Cde.
"	Jacquens Augustine	
"	Richard Brown	
"	William Bell	
"	Henry Bradford	
"	John Bradly	In confinement at Regimental Guard House awaiting trial
		Missing in Action at Jackson La August 3d 1863.
"	Jules Caliste	
"	Henry Clement	In confinement at Regimental Guard House awaiting trial
"	Emile Chatard	Entitled to pay from 20th June to 31st August by over on those rolls
"	Januur J Davis	
"	Ferdinand Fletcher	
"	Francois Fernandez	Absent without leave. Went away Feb 17. 1864
"	Arthur Guillot	
"	Gabriel Gregoir	
"	Charles Hogan	Nurse in Regimental Hospital
	Samuel Hall	In confinement at Regimental Guard House awaiting trial.
"	Richard John	Sick in Regimental Hospital
"	John Johnson	On detached duty at Hd Qrs 1st Div Cde pursuant to Special Orders No 13 dated Jan 17/1864.
"	Anderson John	
"	John Lex	Missing in Action at Jackson La August 3d 1863.
"	Antoine Mathew	Clerk at Corps Hd Qrs.
"	Henry Rita	
"	Joseph Patterson	
"	Victor Bentoiseau	
"	Sam Shepperd	
"	Benjamin String	
"	Henry Singer	
"	Joseph Tompson	
"	Louis Tolein	On daily duty as teamster for R. Q. M.
"	George Ward	
"	Wilbur Walls	
		Was mustered in Company H but immediately transferred to Company F.

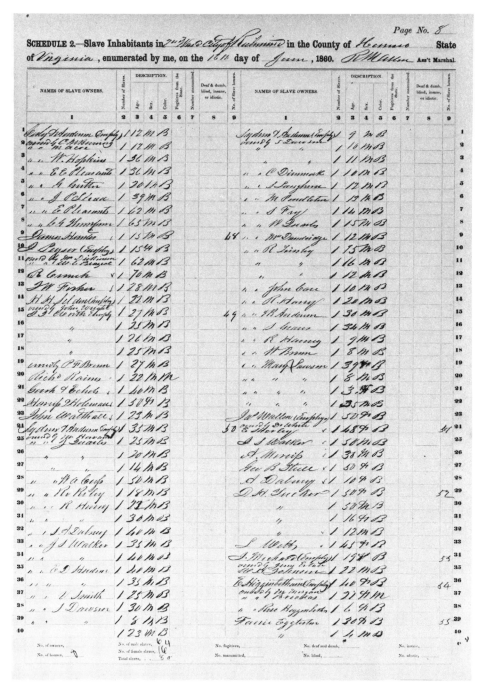

Population census schedules. The population census schedules provide valuable information on the history of blacks. They are used extensively to establish an individual's age and are good sources of black genealogical data. Beginning with the first census (1790), free blacks who were heads of families were listed by their names as were all other free persons. Black slaves in a household were counted but were not listed individually. The 1870 census is an important research source because it was the

SCHEDULE 1.—Free Inhabitants in *The village of New Castle* **in the County of** *Craig* **State of** *Va* **enumerated by me, on the** *19th* **day of** *June* **1860.** *Tobias Wiley* **Ass't Marshal.**

Post Office *New Castle* .

1	2	3	4	5	6	7	8	9	10	11	12	13	14	
Dwelling-houses numbered in the order of visitation.	Families numbered in the order of visitation.	The name of every person whose usual place of abode on the first day of June, 1860, was in this family.	Age.	Sex.	Color: White, black, or mulatto.	Profession, Occupation, or Trade of each person, male and female, over 15 years of age.	Value of Real Estate.	Value of Personal Estate.	Place of Birth, Naming the State, Territory, or Country.	Married within the year.	Attended School within the year.	Persons over 20 years of age who cannot read and write.	Whether deaf and dumb, blind, insane, idiotic, pauper, or convict.	
		Richd H. Hubbard	8	m					Va		/			1
		Maria C. "	5	f					"					2
308	275	David P. Denman	26	m		Waggon Maker	1	500	Va					3
		Callie C. "	25	f					"					4
		Francis "	2	m					"					5
		James N. Whiting	24	m		Day Laborer	1		"					6
		John P. Givens	25	m		Deputy Clerk	1	100	"					7
		Albert Walker	28	m		Merchant	1	2000	"	11				8
		Caroline Armstrong	17	f		Domestic	1		"					9
309	276	Elizabeth Crimes	70	f			1		Va			1		10
		James "	71	m		Day Laborer	1		"			1		11
310	277	Mary A. Calavers	24	f	B	Washer & Ironer	1		Va			1		12
		John A. "	3	m	B				"					13
311	278	Harriet Key	35	f		Domestic	1		Va			1		14
		Thomas O. "	1	m					"					15
312	279	Sarah Raynolds	30	f	B		1		Va					16
		William "	7	m	B				"					17
313	280	Levi Seaber	30	m		Blacksmith	1		Va					18
		Amanda "	29	f					"					19
		Sarah A. "	10	f					"			1		20
		Virginia "	9	f					"					21
		William "	6	m					"					22
		John A. "	3	m					"					23
		Louisa "	1	f					"					24
314	281	Lorenzo R. Dodd	27	m		Teacher Com School	1	2200	Alabama					25
		Harriet P. "	24	f					Va					26
		Isaac C. "	2	m					"					27
		Wilber "	1	m					"					28
315	282	Joseph N. Holt	35	m		Lawyer	2500	500	Va					29
		Naomi "	35	f					"					30
		Maria C. "	11	f					"		1			31
		James N. "	9	m					"		1			32
		Clara N. "	5	m					"					33
		Bettie N. "	3	f					"					34
		Edward J. "	1/2	m					"					35
		John Dooley	12	m	m				"					36
316	283	Thos. H. B. Dillard	32	m		Physician	900		Va					37
		Mary C. "	30	f					"					38
		Albray "	7	m					"			1		39
		Catharine "	4	f					"					40

No. white males,	No. colored males,	No. foreign born,	No. blind,	3,400	5 700	No. Idiotic,	No. convicts,
No. white females,	No. colored females,	No. deaf and dumb,	No. insane,			No. paupers,	

first census taken after the abolition of slavery. As a result, it lists all blacks by name and includes information about all residents of a particular household. The 1870 and 1880 census schedules also include information on former slaves.

Reproduced here are the 1860 and 1870 census schedules. (RG 29, Bureau of the Census)

Inquiries numbered 7, 16, and 17 are not to be asked in respect to infants. Inquiries numbered 11, 12, 15, 16, 17, 19, and 20 are to be answered all merely by an affirmative mark, as /.

SCHEDULE 1.—Inhabitants in 3rd Ward Eufaula T. 11 R 29, in the County of Barbour, State of Ala, enumerated by me on the 9th day of July, 1870.

322

Post Office: Eufaula, Ala.

John A Bassett, Ass't Marshal.

		The name of every person whose place of abode on the first day of June, 1870, was in this family.	Age	Sex	Color	Profession, Occupation, or Trade of each person, male or female.	Value of Real Estate	Value of Personal Estate	Place of Birth, naming State or Territory of U. S.; or the Country, if of foreign birth.	F.	M.	13	14	15	16	17	Whether deaf and dumb, blind, insane, or idiotic.	19	20	
1	2	3	4	5	6	7	8	9	10	11	12	13	14	15	16	17	18	19	20	
1	390 426	Southerland Fannie	45	F	13	Domestic			S.C.	/					/	/				1
2		Sanford Monroe	23	M	13	Domestic			Ga						/	/			1		2
3		Busby Georgiana	23	F	13	Domestic			Ala			/		/	/					3
4		Thomas	1	M	13	Merchant R.	1000	1500	Ala											4
5	391 427	Kendall Jno	44	M	W	Keeping hand			S.C.											5
6		Mary J	36	F	W				S.C.											6
7		Fannie	19	F	W				S.C.			/								7
8		John	9	M	W				Ala			/								8
9		Florence	4	F	W				Ala											9
10		James	3	M	W				Ala											10
11		Marie	3/12	F	W				Ala		Jany									11
12	392 428	Garvin Coleman	57	M	13	Domestic			S.C.						/	/			1		12
13		Scylla	30	F	13	Domestic			Ala						/	/					13
14		Hettie	8	M	13	at School			Ala			/		x						14
15		Flake Mary	40	F	13	Domestic			Fla						/	/					15
16		Florida	4	F	13				Ala											16
17		Bryant Callie	20	F	13	Domestic			Ga						/					17
18	393 429	Peterson Peter	35	M	13	Farm Laborer			Fla						/	/			1		18
19		Ann	30	F	13	Keeping house			S.C.						/	/					19
20		Laura	12	F	13				Ala			/								20
21		Clara	10	F	13				Ala			/		x						21
22		Andrew	8	M	13				Ala			/								22
23		Ola	4	F	13				Ala											23
24		Rodgers Kate	53	F	13	Domestic			Va						/	/					24
25	394 430	Locke Wm H	38	M	W	Dry Goods Merchant R.		600	Ga										1		25
26		Ann J	31	F	W	Keeping house			Ga											26
27		Ella E	13	F	W	at School			Ala			/								27
28		Lula A	11	F	W	at School			Ala			/								28
29		Clifford A	9	M	W	at School			Ala			/								29
30		Nellie L	7	F	W	at School			Ala			/								30
31		Willie H	5	M	W				Ala											31
32		Charles O	3	M	W				Ala											32
33		Pearl	1/12	F	W				Ala		May									33
34		Sylvester Mary	40	F	W				S.C.											34
35	395 431	Cooks Anderson	21	M	13	Domestic			Ala						/				1		35
36		Mandy	14	M	13	Domestic			Ala						/	/					36
37		Lee Sallie	22	F	13	Domestic			Va						/	/					37
38		Tinsly Kate	50	F	13	Domestic			Ga						/	/					38
39		Willis	1	M	13				Ala											39
40	396 432	Brannan Wm 13	57	M	W	Dry Goods Merchant R.	600	300	S.C.										1		40

No. of dwellings, 7. No. of white females, 10. No. of males, foreign born, ___. 16000 2400
" " families, 7. " " colored males, 9. No. of insane, ___. Do. of income.
" " white males, 8. " " female, 11. " " blind, ___. 9 " " ___

Box 114,
Hibland, La.
Jan. 27, 1934.

Mr. Matthew Boyd,
Labor Advisory Board,
Washington, D.C.

Dear Sir,

After reading your article released to the Associated Press for Negroes, I thought I would write to see if you would investigate the condition that prevails in our county in North Louisiana.

You are only admitted to registration for work on the C. W. A. & E. R. A. by a personal appearance or written recommendation of a white man and usually he is allied with a certain political faction.

Whites give names of those they want on payroll exclude rest.

If a survey was made here

Labor Advisory Board letters. These letters reflect some of the problems that arose when the New Dealers' efforts to include blacks in their economic recovery programs encountered racially discriminatory attitudes and practices. (RG 9, National Recovery Administration) you would find the same condition exists as reported in Mississippi.

I will state a typical case. A white lady here was in charge of relief work and owed a colored woman a laundry bill of four dollars & fifty cents.

The one she had employed moved to the county and she went to the one whom she already owed asked her to wash for her, and she told her she already had as many as she could do, and there were three more on relief, who had large families, and the wives could not afford to wash for nothing and they refused, their husbands were cut off directly and were told by the lady in charge their wives ought to have taken the laundry.

I am not asking you to try only to help me personally but my people as a whole.

Thanking you in advance for your consideration.

Respectfully Yours,
(Miss) Lula Lewis.

186

DEPARTMENT OF ECONOMICS

December
Fourth
1934

Mr. Matthew F. Boyd
Labor Adviser
Labor Advisory Board
1126, Investment Bldg.
Washington, D. C.

Dear Mr. Boyd:

I agree with you that if the University would make a
study of the Southern differential it would render a
valuable service. The importance of the topic extends
far beyond the interest of Negro workers as such. Last
summer the Social Science Research Council appropriated
a large sum for a study on the Negro in industry since
the advent of the New Deal. At a meeting held at the
Department of Interior I suggested that the Southern
differential be included in the study but to no avail.

Of course, I cannot speak for the administration but,
as far as my department is concerned I would not undertake such a study until I was assured of adequate
financial support. I am at a loss to understand why
some of the people appointed to look after the interest
of the Negro under the New Deal have not attempted to
make this important study. I mean persons like Mr. Jones
in the Department of Commerce, Mr. Weaver in the Department of Interior and Mr. Oxley in the Department of Labor.

If you are desirous of approaching the President of the
University about the matter I shall be glad to talk over
the matter with you before you see him.

Sincerely yours,

Abram L. Harris, Head

December 21, 1934

Professor Abram L. Harris, Head
Department of Economics
Howard University
Washington, D. C.

Dear Professor Harris:

I do not feel inclined to renew my efforts to have
a real study made of the Southern differential. Some time
ago I spent a great deal of time discussing the matter with
many presumably interested people, and I believe you are
familiar with the efforts that were then made. It seems
to me that in all probability the most effective thing to
do would be for the Presidents of Howard and Tuskegee to
take up the matter with Messrs. Jones, Weaver and Oxley,
work out a definite proposal for the consideration of the
Labor Advisory Board and Secretary Perkins, and thereafter
concentrate upon securing its application.

I am astonished that after seventeen months nothing definite has been done or developed along the lines
of ascertaining the facts in regard to the differential.
While I do not feel that I can take the initiative again,
I shall be very happy to cooperate with anything you may
decide to undertake.

Sincerely yours,

_____

Matthew F. Boyd
Labor Advisory Board

1126, Investment Bldg.
Washington, D. C.

mfb/jg

188

CENSUS of the Freedmen and their descendants of the Cherokee Nation taken by the Commission appointed in the case of Moses Whitmire, Trustee of the Freedmen of the Cherokee Nation vs. The Cherokee Nation and the United States in the Court of Claims at Washington, D.C., the said Commission being composed of William Clifton, William Thompson and Robert H. Kern, the same being made from the testimony taken before said Commission in the Cherokee Nation between May 4th and August 10th, 1896.

First, Authenticated Freedmen and their descendants.

Number.	Name.	Sex.	Age.	District.
1.	Jerry Alberty,	M.	56.	Cooweescoowee.
2.	Ruth Alberty, (wife)	F.	50.	"
3.	Louisa White nee Alberty (daughter)	F.	28.	"
4.	Noah Alberty (son)	M.	26.	"
5.	Moses Alberty (son)	M.	24.	"
6.	Carrie Alberty (daughter)	F.	20.	"
7.	Josh Alberty, Jr. (son)	M.	18.	"
8.	Emory Alberty (son)	M.	16.	"
9.	Millie Alberty (daughter)	F.	15.	"
10.	Sarah or Mary Alberty (daughter)	F.	14.	"
11.	Parsum or Bertha Alberty (daughter)	F.	12.	"
12.	Hattie Alberty (daughter)	F.	5.	"
13.	Estella White (granddaughter)	F.		"
14.	Frank White (grandson)	M.		"

-1-

An 1896 Cherokee census of freedpeople and their descendants. Cherokee and other Indians held Negro slaves who were freed after the Civil War. The freedpeople had the option of becoming citizens of a particular Indian tribe or nation. Later they had to

189

15. Robert Adair,   M.   26.Cooweescoowee.

16. William Adair,   M.   31.   "

17. Ethel Adair (daughter)   F.   7.   "

18. Arizona Adair (daughter)   F.   "

19. Henry Bird,   M.   18.   "

20. Joanna Bird nee Williams (wife)   F.   35.   "

21. William Bird,   M.   20.   "

22. Frances Patterson nee Williams,   F.   56.   "

23. Nancy Williams (daughter)   F.   36.   "

24. Julia Lowe nee Williams (daughter)   F.   24.   "

25. Ellen Duncan (daughter)   F.   22.   "

26. George Williams (son)   M.   20.   "

27. Amanda Williams (daughter)   F.   17.   "

28. Albert Williams (son)   M.   10.   "

29. LeRoy Lowe (grandson)   M.   10.   "

30. Ida Duncan (granddaughter)   F.   3.   "

31. Inola Adair,daughter of Wm.Adair,   F.   3.   "

32. Nevada Adair,daughter of Wm.Adair,   F.   9.   "

33. William Burgess,   M.   43.   "

34. Sarah Burgess (wife)   F.   41.   "

35. Jane Anderson nee Burgess (daughter)   F.   22.   "

36. Maria Burgess (daughter)   F.   17.   "

-2-

prove their citizenship in order to share in the federal grants given to Indians.
Reproduced here is a list of black families that were certified as Cherokee citizens.
(RG 75, Bureau of Indian Affairs)

190

Alleson Day School Choctaw Nation I.T.

Maggie Rolston, teacher   Alleson, I.T. C. Bullard, Supt.

Quarter	No Days	Enrollment					Average Attendance			
		Male	F	M	F	M	Indian	Colored	Indian	Colored
1st Fil 6624/6/07	July Aug Sept	20	2	1	32	24	11		18.7	16.6
2nd 393 17/07	Oct Nov Dec	9	2	1	20	26	7	7	7.1	8.9
3rd 393 17/07	Jan Feb Mar	42	1	1	29	25	8	8	21.2	17.3

Antioch Day School Choctaw Nation I.T.

Lloyd L Gayden, teacher   Lenton, I.T. Colom Bullard, Supt.

							Negro			
							Enrollment		Av. Attend.	
Fil 6624/6/07 1st	Sept Oct	29	2	3	2	15	29	26	14.2	14.6
393 17/07 2nd	Nos Dec	26	5	5	3.3	2.8	13	14	8.2	9.3
393 17/07 3rd	Jan Feb Mar	48					30	34	21	14.6

Leslie M Davies, Teacher   Antlers No. 1 Day School, Choctaw Nation

1st	July Aug Sept						
393 17/07 2nd	Oct Nov Dec	60	24	16	—	—	14.9 9.7
3rd	Jan Feb Mar						
4th	Apr May June						

Extracts from an attendance book of a Choctaw Indian neighborhood school. Some

Blue Ridge Day School, Choctaw Nation

Calom, I.T.

Hattie Ewing teacher

Quarter	No. Days in session	Enrollment Indian		white		Average Attendance Indian		white	
		m	f	m	f	m	f	m	f
6/26/07 1st Quarter — July Aug Sept	20	—	1	30	13	—	.5	18.3	7.8
3.93.7/07 2d Quarter — Oct Nov Dec	60	—	—	19	10	—	—	10.05	7
3.93.7/07 3d Quarter — Jan Feb Mar	42	.1	—	27	25	.9	—	19.1	16.3
4th Quarter — Apr May June									

Boiling Springs Day School, Choctaw Nation

Ft Towson, I.T.

S.B. Witherspoon, teacher

negro

		Enrollment		Aver. Attend.	
		m	f	m	f
6/26/07 1st Quarter — July Aug Sept		12	17	7.5	6.x
3.93.7/07 2d Quarter — Oct Nov Dec	56	11	13	5.9	6.3
3d Quarter — Jan Feb Mar					
4th Quarter — Apr May June					

Baggy Bend Day School, Choctaw Nation

Stringtown, I.T.

J. Leonard Pugh, teacher

negro

		Enrollment		Aver. Attend.	
		m	f	m	f
6/26/07 1st Quarter — July Aug Sept	19	26	24	12.6	12
Hattie Kemp — Oct	22	8	11	3	1.5
3.93.7/07 2d Quarter — Nov Dec	26	9	3	5.08	1.8
3.93.7/07 3d Quarter — Jan Feb Mar	54	19	19	10.8	12.5
4th Quarter — Apr May June					

blacks were educated at schools that were predominantly Indian. These representative pages from a Choctaw attendance book show that the schools were racially segregated.

30

Cedar Day School Choctaw Nation
Lodi, I.T.

Bertha H. Hatcher, teacher

Quarter		No. Days in session	Enrollment				Average Attendance			
			Indian		White		Indian		White	
			M	F	M	F	M	F	M	F
662¼/07 1st Quarter	July Aug Sept	20	7	6	19	13	5	5.4	14.8	10.8
393 17/07 2d Quarter	Oct Nov Dec	36	5	6	17	13	3.5	4.7	8.05	5.6
3d Quarter	Jan Feb Mar									
4th Quarter	Apr May June									

Cedar Grove Day School Choctaw Nation
Sutter, I.T.

Fannie J. Sanders, teacher

		Colored		Non-Col.		Colored		Non-Col.	
		M	F	M	F	M	F	M	F
662¼/07 1st Quarter	July Aug Sept	20	13	7	8	6	9.3	4.7	6.1 3.5
393 17/07 2d Quarter	Oct Nov Dec	60	16	12	7	4	8.05	6.3	3.3 2.6
393 17/07 3d Quarter	Jan Feb Mar	42	18	18	8	6	13.3	10.6	3.9 1.6
4th Quarter	Apr May June								

Cedar Springs Choctaw Nation
Sawyer, I.T.

Carl F. McDonel, teacher

1st Quarter	July Aug Sept	20	2	–	18	12	1.1	–	10.5 9
393 17/07 2d Quarter	Oct Nov Dec	50	2	–	18	18	1.4	–	9.3 12.6
3d Quarter	Jan Feb Mar								
4th Quarter	Apr May June								

The records of the Choctaw schools also provide useful information for possible studies on black education in the Choctaw Nation. (RG 75, Bureau of Indian Affairs)

CHEROKEE AUTHENTICATED ROLL NO.	APPROVED WALLACE ROLL NO.	CLIFTON APPROVED ROLL NO.	OFFICE NO.	NAMES.			AGE.	SEX.	PER CAPITA.	AMOUNT PAID.
				Amount brought forward,						12935 00
15	587	69	74	Downing	Sibedia		41	M	188 75	188 75
16	588	70	75	"	Annie	wife	33	F	188 75	
93	591	73	76	"	Walter	son	16	M	188 75	
	592	74	77	"	Mamie	"	7	M	188 75	
		75	78	"	Maggie	dau	10	F	188 75	
		76	79	"	Liddie	"	3	F	188 75	1134 50
92	590	72	80	"	Henry	son	20	M	188 75	188 75
17	589	71	81	Downing, Luverna		dau	23	F	188 75	188 75
39	649	77	82	Rowe, Lewis			64	M	188 75	
40	650	78	83	"	Chaney	wife	61	F	188 75	377 50
		84	84	"	Wash	gr. son	4	M	188 75	
		85	85	"	Ada	gr. dau	9	F	188 75	377 50
90	656	86	86	Buffington, Florence		"	15	F	188 75	
		87	87	"	Ishmael	son	12	M	188 75	
		88	88	"	Henrietta	dau	9	F	188 75	566 25
		89	89	Rowe,	Jim	son	10	M	188 75	188 75
41	651	79	90	Rowe,	Jeff		34	M	188 75	188 75
42	652	80	91	Rowe,	Eliza		33	F	188 75	188 75
43	653	81	92	Rowe,	Delphia		30	F	188 75	
		179	93	Brakebill, Lewis		son	11	M	188 75	
		180	94	"	Etella	dau	6	F	188 75	
		181	95	"	Ike	son	4	M	188 75	755 00
44	654	82	96	Rowe, Laura			28	F	188 75	188 75
45	655	83	97	Rowe, Martha			25	F	188 75	188 75
				Amount carried forward,						17365 00

Cherokee Freedmen Payroll. This list of Cherokee freedwomen and men were certified as citizens of the Cherokee Nation and were receiving payment from the government of the United States. (RG 75, Bureau of Indian Affairs)

ADDRESS.	SIGNATURES.	DATE OF RECEIPT.	WITNESSES.	REMARKS.
Dist	Zebedee Downing 118580 his mk	Mch 15 1897	Wm J Carey	Exhibit No. 542
				Manuel or Wallace
	Zebedee Downing 1085 his mk	Mch 18 1897	W.G.W. McCrackle Wm J Carey	Exhibit No. 543
	Henry Downing 108644	Mch 19 1897	W.G.W. McCrackle Wm J Carey	Age 65
	Lawrence Downing 137/308 his mark	Mch 16 1897	G Geo Wright Thos J Watts	Exhibit No. 674 Lawrence or Wallace
	Louis Rowe 137476 his mk	Mch 26 1897	W.G.W. McCrackle Wm J Carey	Exhibit No. 800
	Martha Rowe 137439	Mch 25 1897	G Geo Wright Thos J Watts	Exhibit No. 744 Children of 97
	Lewis Rowe 137566 his guardian	Apr 1 '97	W.G.W. McCrackle Wm J Carey	No. 939
"	Eliza L Rowe (Mother) 137373 mark	Mch 22 1897	G Geo Wright Thos J Watts	Exhibit No. 687
	Jess Rowe his 137807 mk	Apl 23 97	Wm J Carey Thos J Watts	Ex. No. 1179
	Eliza L Rowe 137373 mark	Mch 22 1897	G Geo Wright Thos J Watts	Exhibit No. 687
				now Brakebill
	Sophia Rowe 108527 1085	Mch 17 1897	W.G.W. McCrackle Wm J Carey	Exhibit No. 487
	Laura Rowe 1085	Mch 17 1897	W.G.W. McCrackle Wm J Carey	Exhibit No. 500
	Martha Rowe 137433	Mch 25 1897	G Geo Wright Thos J Watts	Exhibit No. 744

Gen. O.O. Howard, commissioner of the Bureau of Refugees, Freedmen, and Abandoned Lands, 1882. The Audiovisual Archives Division of the National Archives maintains still photographs, motion pictures, and sound recordings that document the history of our nation—valuable sources for research on Afro-American history. (Audiovisual Archives Division; Brady Collection, no. 111-BA-2156)

Record for Sarah Pryor

No. 198

Date of Application, July 19/70
Where born, Richmond, Va
Where brought up, do
Residence, Cor 3ᵈ & Clay
Age, about 27
Complexion, Dark brown
Occupation, } keeps house
Works for }
Wife, Husband — John Pryor
Children, none

Father, }
       } dead
Mother, }
Brothers, Charles Smith
Sisters, none

Signature, Unable to write

Record Caroline Bowie

No. 4500

Date of Application, Mch 13/72
Where born, Georgia
Where brought up, "
Residence, Annunciation bet 1ˢᵗ &
                                   Philip
Age, 29.
Complexion, Light
Occupation, Nurse
Works for
Wife or husband, dead — Joseph Bowie
Children, dead, Robin   died in Ga

Father, Claiborne Edwards —
Mother, dead, Nancy
Brothers, Geo Wash McIntosh, Sugean Edwds
          Octavus Augustus Edwds, Claiborne Julius,
          Paul Warren, Claiborne Summum
Sisters, } Mary Elizabeth (Johnny, Willie —
         } Anna Love   (all Edwards
         } Nancy —   (except 1ˢᵗ one

In case of death — Her father can draw
                              and Nancy can draw
                                 in case of her
Signature, Can't write   fathers death

Depositors' signature books. The Freedmen's Savings and Trust Company was incorporated by Congress in 1865. The main office was located in Washington, D.C., but by 1870 thirty-three branches had been established in cities throughout the country. Each branch kept a register with information about depositors. These pages from selected registers reveal the wide range of information that is found in such records. (RG 101, Comptroller of the Currency)

OVERLEAF:
Diplomatic and consular dispatches. As members of the consular service and Diplomatic Corp, blacks represented their government in a number of foreign posts. Their correspondence with the Department of State as well as other communications deal with the relationship between the two governments. The records also include reports on the domestic affairs of the host countries. (RG 59, Department of State)

Legation of the United States.
Port au Prince, Haiti, December 6th 18,,

Honorable
William M. Evarts,
Secretary of State,
Washington, U.S.A.

Sir:

As regards the condition of things in
San Domingo, the neighboring Republic of Haiti,
I have learned from what I deem a reliable source
that there exist there three parties engaged really,
directly or indirectly, in the revolutionary movements
at present progressing in that country.

Baez, the President of the Republic, with his
Minister of War, Pablo Villanueva, and his chief
general, Jose Maria Camunero, with a government
force numbering from two to three thousand men,
known as the "Reds", favoring annexation and
progress in all those things which pertain to the
moral and material welfare of the people, seems
able to meet and defeat those who seek to overthrow
the Government.

Luperon, a leader of one of the factions of the
people, said to be an able and daring man, of great

force

force of character, with some two or three hundred followers, as yet neither organized nor armed, but designated and described as the "Blues", favoring like Baez annexation and progress, is inclined to unite his forces with those of the Government. If this be true, since the forces of the Government are said to be loyal and firm as well as brave, the President must prove invincible, and the Government be sustained.

Gonzales, opposing both annexation and progress, insisting upon the payment of all national debts before incurring others, with a force numbering from three to five hundred, lead by Isidoro Ortea, a young and dashing officer, and known as the "Greens", attempts the overthrow of Baez. His movement would seem to be a determined one, conducted with vigor and pertinacity. It is reported that he has the sympathy of the Haitien Government; and that he receives from it, also, material aid.

I cannot do more as far as this subject is concerned than to give report. "Le Moniteur", the organ of the Haitien Government, of this date, announces the return of the Minister of War and Marine, who has been absent, from the Capital some four weeks upon a man of war cruising in

the

the neighborhood of Cape Haitien, near the border line between the two countries, in the following terms, as translated: ___

"General Auguste Montas, Minister of War and Marine arrived Tuesday evening at Port au Prince after having accomplished to the satisfaction of the Chief of State, the important mission which had been entrusted to him in the North." ___

What "the important mission" was is not stated. It is to be hoped that it had no connection with revolutionary movements in San Domingo.

I am informed that the troops of Baez are in good condition, loyal and firm, and armed with the Remington rifle. His Minister of War and chief general are said to be brave men.

The promptness and vigor employed in the recapture of Puerto Plata, taken and held for three days by Gonzales, indicate that these statements are true. I have been informed that the troops of the Government, when some weeks ago the insurgents captured Puerto Plata, taking refuge in the forts, opened a random fire upon the city, cannon balls striking houses indiscriminately, killing and wounding natives and foreigners; no proper discrimination

being

being observed even as to the sacred and invio-
lable rights and privileges of our Consul residing
there. Indeed I have just learned that he has felt
it to be his duty in view of his insecurity to leave,
and is now on his way home.

Gonzales is said to be intending to attack
Santo Domingo City and to besiege Santiago. He
is exhibiting such determination and vigor that
the impression seems to be gaining ground in spite
of the facts already stated that the revolutionists
must succeed ere long; Baez be overthrown; and
the leader of the insurrectionary forces become his
successor in the Government.

I do not present the facts and statements herein submitted as absolutely reliable. I believe them,
however, to be substantially correct; and they have
come to my knowledge in such manner, and from
such source, and seem to be of such character and
importance, as to justify prompt communication

I have the honor to be, Sir, most respectfully,

Your Obedient Servant,
John Mercer Langston

No. 123 Confidential-Diplomatic.

Legation of the United States
Port au Prince, Haiti, January 29, 1891.

Mr. Frederick Douglass to the Secretary of State.

Subject
Conference with the Haitian Government concerning the Mole St. Nicolas

Synopsis.
Conference held at National Palace Jan. 27, to discuss request made by the United States for a lease of the Mole St. Nicolas as a naval coaling station.

No. 123 Confidential Diplomatic.

Legation of the United States
Port au Prince, Haiti, January 29, 1891.

Honorable
James G. Blaine,
Secretary of State,
Washington, U.S.A.

Sir:
I have the honor to inform you that on Monday, the 26th instant, I was invited by Rear Admiral Bancroft Ghe-rardi and went on board of the United States war steamer "Philadelphia," which cast anchor in this harbor on the morning of the 26th instant, and arrived on board of her I

received

202

received from him your full
instructions as to the wishes
of the President of the United
States in regard to receiving
from the Government of Haiti, a coaling station for our
naval vessel at the Mole
St. Nicolas.

In pursuance of these
instructions I sought and
obtained an interview with
Mr. Firmin, the Minister of
Foreign Affairs, on Tuesday
morning, the 27th instant, and
stated to him the desire of Admiral Gherardi and myself
to have an early meeting
with President Hyppolite and
himself, and asked him to
inform

inform me at his earliest
convenience of the time which
would be agreeable to him
for that purpose.

Mr. Firmin readily agreed
to arrange the matter, and on
Wednesday, the 28th instant,
I received from him a note
stating that His Excellency the
President of Haiti would receive Admiral Gherardi
and myself at the Palace at
four o'clock in the afternoon
of the same day.

At the hour thus appoint-
ed, Admiral Gherardi, Lieu-
tenant Keise and myself
went to the Palace. We were
there received by Mr. Firmin
and

and conducted to a spacious
room, in the center of which was
a table with chairs for five persons, President Hyppolite, Minister Firmin, Rear Admiral
Gherardi, Lieut Keise being
seated, President Hyppolite soon entered the
room and gave us a cordial
greeting, after which, without
loss of time, I said.

"Mr. President, aside from
"the grateful duty of paying
"our respects to your Excellen-
"cy, we have an important
"matter to bring to your at-
"tention, which Rear Admiral
"Gherardi, who has been es-
"pecially commissioned by the
                            "United

"United States Government for the purpose will present and explain.

In response to my remark the President inclined his head when Admiral Ghevardi suc- ceeded to make known the wishes of our Government in the matter of obtaining a loan of the State at Nicolay for the purpose already mentioned, reminding the President of ur- vices rendered of the friend- ship shown for his Govern- ment by the United States, and of certain promises made by the Haitian Provisional Government, which now it was the desire of the Govern- ment

ment at Washington to have fulfilled.

It is due to Rear Admi- ral Ghevardi to say that he met the requirements of the occasion in a mas- terly manner. His present- ation and marked by skill and ability.

There was little left for me to present in the line of fact or in the citing of special obligations. I therefore con- tented myself with treating the application as a very sim- ple one that might be rea- sonably complied with by a friendly, neighboring nation. I invited attention to the facts that

that the repugnance to seal- ing any part of Haitian ter- ritory to a foreign power grew out of conditions which had long since ceased to exist and that the policy of Ex- clusion, once a source of saf- ety, was now, under altered conditions, a source of danger.

The speaking was not con- fined to one side. Mr. Firmin considered the subject under two heads, first, as an obli- gation created by certain obli- gations performed and promises made by the Provisional Govern- ment of General Hyppolite, and, secondly, as a simple application from one friendly power

Governor to another for a she-
cial accommodation. Under
the first head Mr. Firman
did not accept in all its
force and effect, the statement of facts made by Ad-
miral Gherardi and sought
to qualify and limit the significance of these facts. He
however said that while
as an individual he was
in favor of granting the
lease, he was compelled to
treat the subject as an officer of the Government.
The interview lasted three
hours and was marked by
earnestness on both sides. It
was terminated by an as-
surance

that the Executive
department of the Haitien
Government would grant the
lease asked for, subject to its
ratification by the Legislative chambers.
The details of the said
lease are to be prepared by
Admiral Gherardi and my
self.

I am, sir,
your obedient servant,
Bancroft Gherardi

205

Virginia State College
Petersburg, Virginia

EXTENSION DEPARTMENT

2 March 1949

Dr. Ambrose Caliver
Specialist for Higher Education of Negroes,
Adviser on Related Problems
U. S. Office of Education
Washington 25, D. C.

Dear Dr. Caliver:

Thank you for inviting me to attend the meeting of the National Advisory Committee on the Education of Negroes, to be held in Philadelphia on March 29. President Foster has indicated that I shall be permitted to attend the meeting. I shall therefore appreciate any information which you may send so that I may make preparation for this meeting. Will this particular meeting be of one day's duration?

There are two problems affecting Negro adults, as I see it, which increasingly demand the application of the principles and methods of guidance. One of the major problems is that of vocational guidance. In order that Negroes might be better prepared for the acquisition of and maintenance of economic security, it will be necessary that effective assistance be provided in the area of vocational guidance. There is an urgent need for scientific aid in regard to the selection of, the preparation for, entering upon and progressing in an occupation. The need for constant vocational adjustment due to technological changes and the fact that a wider variety of vocational opportunities are becoming available for Negroes have made the need for guidance in the area of vocations more and more important.

An example of two types of services being rendered to adults on a limited scale are the adult consultative services which are carried on under the supervision of the Department of Education in Virginia, and the Guidance Centers under the supervision of the Veterans Administration in various areas for veterans. In the event that an activity of this kind could be extended on a more representative scale, there should certainly be competent Negroes on the consultative staff.

The second problem is counselling services in home and family life. It seems to me that services in this area giving primary emphasis to husband and wife relationships and parent and child relationships could do much to reduce the number of broken families and the increasing amount of maladjustment among adolescents.

I am making no effort here to go into these problems in great detail. I should be glad to set forth in a more detailed manner, if necessary, my personal opinions as to the principles and methods of guidance which may be employed in working toward a solution of these problems.

Very truly yours,

Albert T. Harris

Albert T. Harris
Director of Extension

ATH:J

U.S. Office of Education correspondence on blacks and education. These letters delineate the many efforts of black education specialists to encourage higher education among blacks. They also describe the professional services that black colleges provided. (RG 12, Office of Education)

Virginia State College
Petersburg, Virginia

July 27, 1950

Dr. Ambrose Caliver
Specialist of Higher Education of Negroes and
Director, Project for Adult Education of Negroes
Federal Security Agency
Office of Education
Washington 25, D. C.

My dear Dr. Caliver:

Thank you for the kindness of the copy of your letter of
July 24 to Dr. Eichelberger in reference to assistance with the
Quadrennial Session of the General Convention on Christian Education
of the African M. E. Zion Church, in Richmond, Virginia, August 1-6.

We deeply appreciate your kindness in recommending our services
to Dr. Eichelberger.

Sincerely yours,

Samuel A. Madden, Director
Audio-Visual Center

SAM/ebc

P.S. We think we should let you know, and hope
to secure also your blessings, that we
purpose (and have been granted) a leave
of absence for this school year to
study. We'll return to Columbia, Teachers
College. We hope to make a real
start toward the Ph.D. - D.Ed.
Sam

207

The Center for Cartographic and Architectural Archives of the National
Archives maintains archives from many federal agencies which document
the history of our nation. Among these permanently valuable
cartographic archives are maps that contain information on the history of
Afro-Americans. This selection only suggests the variety of information
found in such archival holdings. In most instances, they are one-of-a-
kind, but the availability of these records provides still another dimension
to federal archives as sources for Afro-American studies.

Trend of black population in census tracts of New York City, 1920-1930. (RG 31,
Federal Housing Administration)

Spread of black population in the District of Columbia, 1920-1930. (RG 31, Federal Housing Administration)

Percent of dwelling units occupied by nonwhites in the District of Columbia, 1934. (RG 31, Federal Housing Administration)

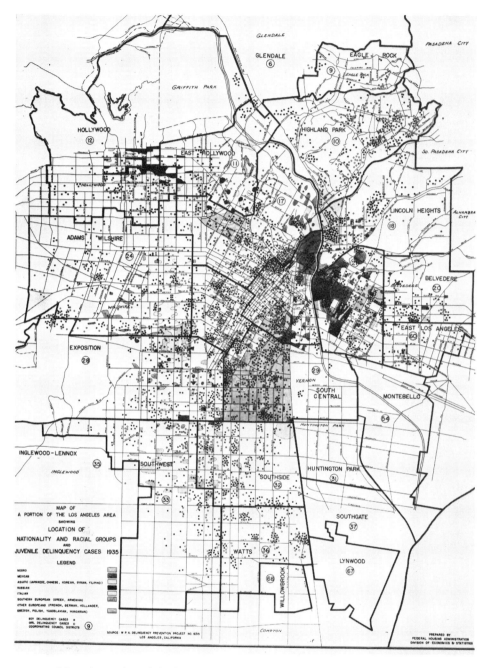

Map of a portion of the Los Angeles area showing location of nationality and racial groups and juvenile delinquency cases, 1935. (RG 31, Federal Housing Administration)

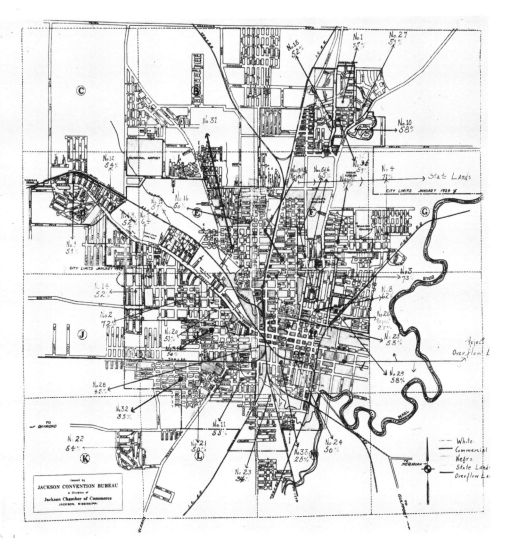

Population trend of blacks and whites in Jackson, Mississippi, 1930. The original map is color coded. (RG 31, Federal Housing Administration)

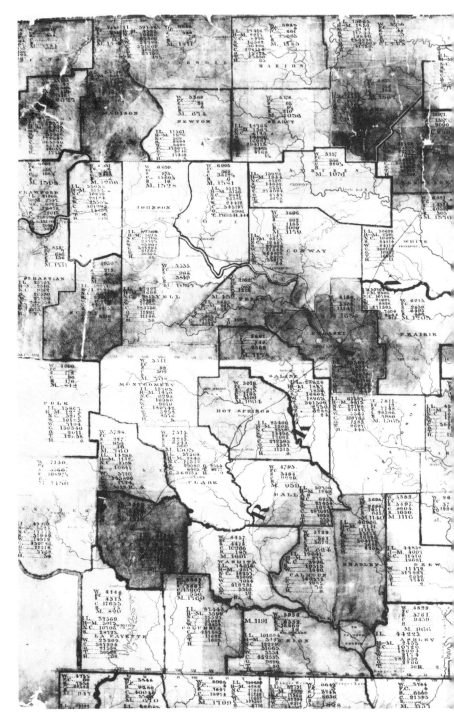

Map of Mississippi, Louisiana, and Arkansas showing the population distribution of whites, free colored, and slaves. (RG 57, Geological Survey)

Map of
MISSISSIPPI,
LOUISIANA & ARKANSAS
Exhibiting The
Post Offices, Post Roads, Canals, Rail Roads, &c.
BY
David H. Burr
Late Topographer to the Post Office
Geographer to the House of Representatives of the U.S.

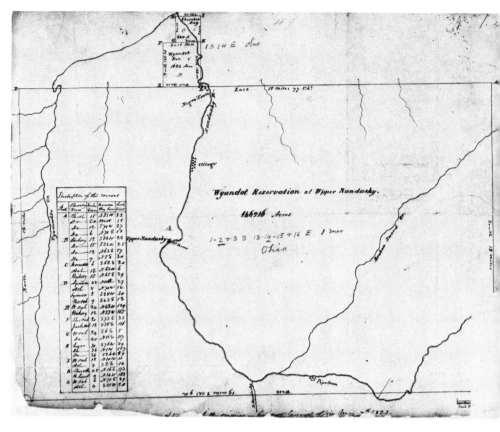

This map shows the location of a Negro town on the Ohio Sandusky River, 1823. (RG 49, Bureau of Land Management)

214

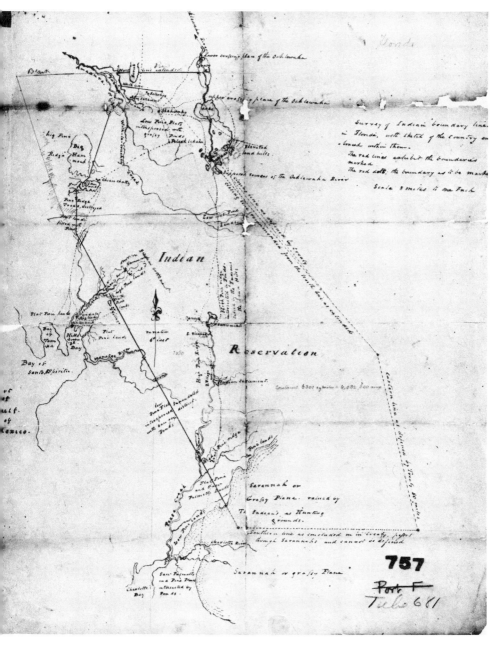

Undated map of an Indian reservation near Tampa, Florida, showing the location of a Negro settlement. (RG 75, Bureau of Indian Affairs)

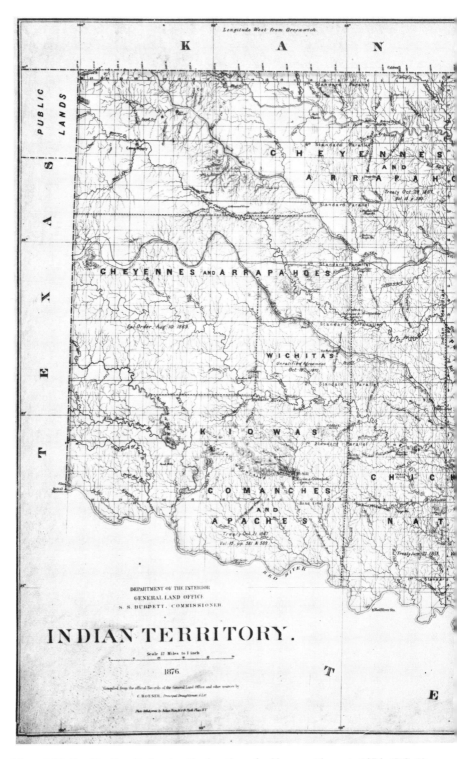

Map of "Indian Territory" showing the location of a Negro settlement, 1876. (RG 49, Bureau of Land Management)

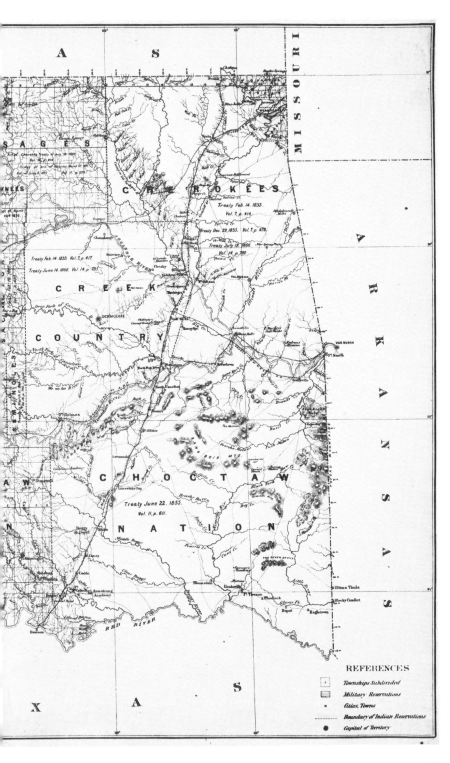

REFERENCES

Townships Subdivided
Military Reservations
Cities, Towns
Boundary of Indian Reservations
Capital of Territory

Biographical Sketches
of Contributors

Preston E. Amos

A graduate of Morehouse College and Atlanta University, Preston Amos is presently serving as foreign service information officer, United States Information Agency. His assignments have included senior writer in the Voice of America's News Division; information center director in Damascus, Syria; assistant cultural affairs officer, Lahore, Pakistan; binational center director and public affairs officer, Belo Horizonte, Brazil; librarian, Milwaukee Public Library; and head librarian, Delaware State College. Currently writing a book on seventy-odd black recipients of the Congressional Medal of Honor, he is also author of *Above and Beyond in the West: Black Medal of Honor Winners, 1870-1890*.

Mary Frances Berry

Educated at Howard University, the University of Michigan, and the University of Michigan Law School, Dr. Mary Frances Berry is professor of history and law and a senior fellow in the Institute for the Study of Educational Policy at Howard University. She also serves as commissioner and vice chair of the U.S. Commission on Civil Rights. From 1977 to 1980 she served as assistant secretary for education in the Department of Health, Education, and Welfare and was formerly the chancellor of the University of Colorado, Boulder, where she held an appointment as professor of history and law. Her professional appointments have included assistant professor of history, Central Michigan University; associate professor, University of Maryland; adjunct associate professor, University of Michigan; and provost of the Division of Behavioral and Social Sciences, University of Maryland. She has been a consultant for the Department of Housing and Urban Development; the Office for Civil Rights, Health, Education, and Welfare; and the U.S. Civil Rights Commission. Berry is also a member of the District of Columbia Bar. In addition to numerous articles on constitutional and legal history, she is the author of *Black*

Resistance, White Law: A History of Constitutional Racism in America; Military Necessity and Civil Rights Policy: Black Citizenship and the Constitution, 1861-1868; and *Stability, Security, and Continuity: Mr. Justice Burton and Decision-Making in the Supreme Court, 1945-58.*

Andrew Billingsley

Educated at Grinnell College, Boston University, University of Michigan, and Brandeis University, Dr. Billingsley is presently serving as president of Morgan State University. His professional appointments have included vice president for academic affairs and professor of sociology, Howard University; assistant chancellor for academic affairs, University of California; associate professor of social welfare, University of California; assistant dean of students, University of California; and social worker and research assistant, Massachusetts Society for the Prevention of Cruelty to Children. He has received numerous research grants and awards, including the Biannual National Association of Social Workers Research Award (1964), Social Science Fellowship (1968), and the Michael Schwerner Memorial Award (1969). He has contributed articles to numerous scholarly journals and publications and is the author of *Black Families in White America* and *Children of the Storm* (coauthored with Jeanne Giovannovi).

John W. Blassingame

Educated at Fort Valley State College, Howard University, and Yale University, Dr. Blassingame has served as editor of the Frederick Douglass Papers since 1973. He has been acting chairperson, Afro-American Studies, Yale University; and assistant editor of the Booker T. Washington Papers, University of Maryland. Some of his published essays and articles include: "The Freedom Fighters"; "American Nationalism and Other Loyalties in the Southern Colonies, 1963-1975"; "The Press and American Intervention in Haiti and the Dominican Republic, 1904-1920"; "Sambos and Rebels: The Character of the Southern Slave"; "Bibliographical Essay: Foreign Writers View Cuban Slavery"; and "The Afro-Americans: From Mythology to Reality." He edited *New Perspectives on Black Studies;* coedited *In Search of America;* and with Louis Harlan coedited *The Autobiographical Writings of Booker T. Washington.* He is also author of *The Slave Community, Black New Orleans, 1860-1880,* and *Slave Testimony.*

Barry A. Crouch

Receiving his education at the University of Wyoming and the University of New Mexico, Dr. Crouch was a member of the faculty of Bowie State College, Bowie, Maryland, from 1974 until 1979, serving as assistant professor of history. He is now assistant professor of history at Gallaudet College in Washington, D.C. He has been awarded research grants by the National Endowment for the Humanities and the American Philosophical Society, and was an editing fellow in 1972-1973 with the Booker T. Washington Papers at the University of Maryland. Crouch is completing a manuscript on blacks in Texas during and after the Civil War and has published several articles in various journals, including *Civil War History* and *Prologue: The Journal of the National Archives.*

Marilyn Cynthia Greene

A graduate of Howard University, Marilyn Cynthia Greene is presently the director of Workshops for Careers in the Arts at George Washington University. Her professional appointments have included administrator, Faculty Research Program in Social Sciences and research assistant, Office of the Vice President for Academic Affairs, Howard University; administrative assistant, Urban Economic Development Systems, Berkeley, California; executive secretary to Sidney Poitier and producer, Joe Glickman; and project specialist, Secondary Teacher Education Program, Stanford University. She has also done extensive sociological and historical research with emphases on black and female minorities. Her articles have appeared in several scholarly journals. Her articles include: "Expressions of Black Women in the Antebellum Period in America" (coauthor with Andrew Billingsley), "Mainstream: Acculturation of Free Blacks in the Ante- and Post-Bellum Eras," and "Black Arts and Humanities" (coauthor with Andrew Billingsley).

Herbert G. Gutman

Educated at Queens College, Columbia University, and the University of Wisconsin, Herbert Gutman is a professor of history at the Graduate Center, City University of New York. A former member of the Executive Board of the Organization of American Historians, he also represented the American Historical Association on the National Historical Publications and Records Commission. His academic appointments have included Social Science Research Council fellow, University of Wisconsin; instructor of history, Fairleigh Dickinson University; associate professor, State University of New York; and professor, University of Rochester. He has contributed articles to numerous scholarly journals, including *American Historical Review, Annals, Labor History, Political Science Quarterly,* and *Trans-Action.* Gutman is the author of *Slavery and the Numbers Game: A Critique of Time on the Cross; Work, Culture, and Society in Industrializing America;* and the *Black Family in Slavery and Freedom, 1750-1925.* He is completing a study of the emancipated slaves during and after the Civil War and is presently at work on a social history of working people in America.

Alex Haley

Alex Haley was born August 11, 1921, in New York, and was reared in Henning, Tennessee, the oldest of three sons of a father who taught at southern black colleges, and a mother who taught at grammar schools. Finishing high school at fifteen, Haley attended college for two years and, in 1939, he enlisted in the U.S. Coast Guard. He served first as a messboy and, in 1952, advanced to chief journalist.

In 1959 Haley retired from the Coast Guard and entered a new career of full-time writing. He wrote as a free-lancer for numerous magazines, including *Harper's, Altantic Monthly,* and *New York Times.* He has served as a staff writer for *Reader's Digest* and as a chief interviewer for *Playboy* magazine.

A succession of headline personalities interviewed for *Playboy* by Haley included the controversial Malcolm X. Haley worked two years interviewing him and writing *The Autobiography of Malcolm X,* which was published in 1965. The book has sold over four and one-half million copies, in eight languages; it has been named among the "Ten Best American Books of the 1960s Decade." Haley's other awards have included the honorary academic degree of Doctor of Letters.

Since then, Haley has engaged in a long, intensive, and challenging research. Pursuing across five years and three continents a few slender, oral history, family lineage clues passed down to him in Tennessee by his maternal grandmother, Haley finally actually has traced that side of his family back to a Mandingo youth named Kunta Kinte, from the small village of Juffure, The Gambia, West Africa. He has now written the resulting book, which is entitled *Roots.* The honors received by Haley for

Roots include a resolution of tribute passed by the United States Senate on March 14, 1977 and a special Pulitzer Prize awarded on April 18, 1977.

Haley is a popular lecturer in national demand and has taught courses in black heritage at the University of California at Berkeley.

J.C. James

A graduate of Talladega College of Alabama, J.C. James received his M.A. from Boston University. He did further work in history and government at Harvard and American universities. He has served as a member of the staff of the Massachusetts Historical Records Survey; professor of history and government, Tennessee A and I University; archivist, National Archives and Records Service; associate director of admissions, Howard University; program officer, Office of Civil Rights, Department of Health, Education, and Welfare; chief, Division of Equal Educational Opportunities in the U.S. Office of Education; director, Franklin D. Roosevelt Library.

In 1969 he investigated the status of black school administrators under desegregation programs and published his findings in an article entitled "The Black Principal: Another Vanishing American."

W. Augustus Low

A graduate of Lincoln University (Missouri) and the University of Iowa, Dr. Low has served as professor of history at the University of Maryland, Baltimore County since 1966. His writings have appeared in many reputable publications. He became editor of the *Journal of Negro History* in 1970.

Roland C. McConnell

Receiving his education at Howard University and New York University, Dr. McConnell joined the professional staff of the National Archives in 1943 and served in the War Records Branch from 1943-1947. He has been a member of the faculty of Morgan State University since 1947, serving as professor of history since 1948 and as chairperson of the Department of History from 1967-1975. McConnell has directed two workshops on Negro history and materials under the joint auspices of the university and the

National Endowment for the Humanities and has served as a member of the Executive Board of the Association for the Study of Afro-American Life and History and as research consultant for the Afro-American Bicentennial Committee, Washington, D.C. His publications include *Negro Troops of Antebellum Louisiana: A History of the Battalion of Free Men of Color* and biographical sketches of Robert Purvis, Archibald Grimké, Thurgood Marshall, Louis Stokes, and Roy Wilkins in the McGraw Hill, *Encyclopedia of World Biography*, volumes 1 through 12, 1973.

Harold T. Pinkett

Educated at Morgan State University, the University of Pennsylvania, Columbia University, and American University, Dr. Pinkett held several staff and supervisory positions at the National Archives from 1942 to 1979. He retired as chief of the Legislative and Natural Resources Branch of this agency. He has been a lecturer in the Department of History at Howard University and American University. He has been a member of the Editorial Board of the *Journal of Negro History* and is presently a member of the District of Columbia Historical Records Advisory Board. His professional activities have also included editorship of the *American Archivist* (1968-71), coeditorship of *Research in the Administration of Public Policy,* and publication of *Gifford Pinchot, Private and Public Forester,* as well as numerous articles on archival and historical subjects.

Elaine M. Smith

A graduate of Bethune-Cookman College, Elaine Smith received her M.A. degree from Boston University and has done further graduate study at the University of Maryland and Howard University. She is presently serving as assistant professor of history, Alabama State University, Montgomery. Her professional appointments have included research assistant, Program for the Disadvantaged and Handicapped, U.S. Office of Education, Department of Health, Education, and Welfare; educational program specialist, U.S. Office of Education; and history instructor, Tuskegee Institute, Alabama. In 1963 she received the Woodrow Wilson Fellowship and in 1965 was listed in *Outstanding Young Women in America*. Her research and writings have been on Mary McLeod Bethune.

Edgar A. Toppin

Educated at Howard University and Northwestern Univeristy, Dr. Toppin is presently a professor of history at Virginia State College. His professional appointments have included history instructor, Alabama State College; associate professor, University of Akron; instructor on the educational television series "Americans from Africa: A History"; instructor on the CBS Black Heritage series; scriptwriter-consultant, Bicentennial Radio Network; consultant-researcher, "Red, White, and Blue in Black" on Black Mutual Radio Network; member of Board of Directors, Southern Fellowship Fund; member of Board of Directors, Fayetteville United Fund; member of World Book Encyclopedia Social Science Advisory Committee; and visiting professor at several colleges and universities. In addition to numerous contributions to historical journals, he is also the author of *A Mark Well Made, Blacks in America: Then and Now; A Biographical History of Blacks in America since 1528; The Black American in United States History; Pioneers and Patriots* (coauthored with Lavinia Dobler); and *The Unfinished March* (coauthored with Carol Drisko).

Okon Edet Uya

Okon Edet Uya received his B.A. degree from the University of Ibadan in 1966, his M.A. in 1968 and his Ph.D. in 1969, both from the University of Wisconsin. He is currently professor of history, University of Nigeria at Calabar. His academic appointments have included visiting assistant professor of history, Beloit College; special consultant on African/Afro-American Studies, Extension Division, University of Wisconsin; telelecturer, Selected Topics in African History, Berea College; visiting assistant professor of history, University of Wisconsin; consultant, Afro-American History Workshop, Wisconsin State University; associate professor of history, Afro-American Studies Department, University of Wisconsin; and associate professor, African Studies and Research Program, Howard University. His publications include: *From Slavery to Public Service: Robert Smalls, 1839-1915; Black Brotherhood; Afro-Americans and Africa; Black Civilizations: A Cultural History of Black People in Africa and the New World,* coauthor with John Willis and Tony Morrison; *Prelude to Disaster: An Analysis of the Racial Policies of Boer and British Settlers in South Africa before 1910; Americans from Africa: An Independent Study Guide;* and *Problems of African Historiography.*

James D. Walker

James Walker was, until his retirement in 1979, a genealogical and local history specialist at the National Archives. His career at the Archives began in 1944. He has lectured at workshops, forums, classes, and seminars, and other programs in the United States and Canada. In 1977 he served as president of the Afro-American Historical and Genealogical Society. He is a member of the councils of the American Association for State and Local History and the National Genealogical Society. A renowned genealogy lecturer and consultant, he is the author of *Black Genealogy: How to Begin.*

Index

Abbott, Robert S., 102

Adjutant General's Office: records of, 4, 44 (facsimile of Civil War documents), 45, 66, 67

Afro-American League, 36

Afro-American spirituals, 124-125

"Alabama's Soldier Experiment, 1898-1899" (Gatewood), *Journal of Negro History*, 4

Alexander, Will W., 102, 106

American Historical Association: and the National Archives, 10, 113

American Missionary Association, 89

"American Negro Maritime War Effort, Sun Shipyard No. 4, 1942-45" (Wright), 45

American University: and the National Archives, 168

Amos, Preston E., 65, 219

Andrews, Charles, 10

Anthony (no last name), 142

Aptheker, Herbert, 118

Arkansas: population distribution of whites, free coloreds, and slaves in, 214 (map)

Army Commands, 1784-1821: records of, 45

Army of the Potomac, 65

Arthur, Chester Alan, 61

Association for the Study of Afro-American Life and History. *See* Association for the Study of Negro Life and History

Association for the Study of Negro Life and History, 104, 165, 168; 1949 annual meeting, 42

Atlanta University, 103, 124

Autobiography of Malcolm X (Haley), 148

Badger (Gen.), 62

Baker, Edward Lee, 73 n. 1

Barnett, Ross: recorded interview with, 108

Bassett, Ebenezer D., 20

Battle of New Orleans: Blacks in, 43

Battle of the Crater: Blacks in, 65

Bell, Whitefield, 116

Ben (no last name), 142

Berkhofer, Robert F., Jr., 28

Bernhard, Berl: papers of, 108; recorded interview with, 108

Berry, Mary Frances, 35, 53, 54, 55, 219-220; *Black Resistance, White Law*, 53

Bethune-Cookman College, 48

Bethune Foundation, 49

Bethune, Mary McLeod, 47, 48 (portrait), 48-52, 103, 104, 105, 115; audiovisual records on, 51; and Federal Council on Negro Affairs, 49; and Lyndon B. Johnson, 53; and National Association of Colored Women, 48-49; and National Council of Negro Women, 49; and National Youth Administration, 49-52; sources of data on, 51

Billingsley, Andrew, xvii, 123, 159, 160, 161, 220; *Black Families in White America*, 124

Billington, Monroe, "Civil Rights, President Truman and the South," *Journal of Negro History*, 3

Billington, Roy Allen, 22, 23

"Black Cabinet." *See* Federal Council on Negro Affairs

Black Families in White America (Billingsley), 124

Black family life: among freemen and women, 126-128; existence questioned, 124-125; marriage records as evidence of, 130-134, 135-137 (tables); patterns of extended, 159; in slavery, 123-138, 159-160; on smaller farms, 123; sources of data on, 124, 140; role of

227